D0850992

Salvation in
Fresh Perspective

Salvation in
Fresh Perspective

Covenant, Cross, and Kingdom

Matthew I. Ayars

WIPF & STOCK · Eugene, Oregon

Wipf & Stock
An Imprint of Wipf and Stock Publishers
199 W. 8th Ave., Suite 3
Eugene, OR 97401

www.wipfandstock.com

ISBN 13: 978-1-4982-0182-7

Manufactured in the U.S.A.

For Stacey
Wife, best friend, inspiration

Contents

Author's Preface

THIS BOOK WAS AN accident. In the midst of writing my doctoral dissertation, I made the mistake of reading *Justification: God's Plan, Paul's Vision* by N. T. Wright. Many friends and colleagues had suggested that I read Tom Wright, but my doctoral studies had me under a pile of books on Hebrew poetry, linguistics, and literary theory. Finally, I downloaded a sample of *Justification* just to see what the hype was all about. I read the sample in about fifteen minutes, immediately downloaded the entire book, and scarfed that thing down like a Cinnabon. I was hooked.

As Wright methodically unpacked his reading of Paul while keeping the text and its first-century Judaic context central, I became convinced that he was right. Not only this, but I also began to wonder if what he was saying about Luther and his reading of Paul (through sixteenth-century eyes) could also be true of John Wesley and his reading of Paul. I began to prayerfully realize that Wesley's reading was deeply shaped by his own personal sin crisis and is deeply concerned with the purity of the heart of the individual. Paul is concerned about this too, but was this *central* to what Paul was saying? What about Israel? What about covenant? What about the kingdom that the Gospel writers insist is at the center of the gospel message? I started looking for answers. My reading was centered in the New Perspective but also went beyond there.

As I was on family vacation taking a break from the mission field as well as my dissertation writing, I began processing my thoughts by putting notes to paper. After a short time I had 40,000 words. What started out as a small area of interest consumed me. I began to see with greater clarity the need in mainstream Christianity for an appeal to remember that salvation and the Gospel is about much more than substitutionary atonement and an escape from final judgment.

As a seminary president in Haiti, I have lots of opportunities to preach. As I would prayerfully prepare sermons, the Holy Spirit continued to bring me back to preaching and teaching this full, wholly integrated, and deeply biblical Gospel. I would sense his leading to remind folks that while substitutionary atonement and the individual sin crisis is an important aspect of the Gospel, there's more to the story; there is covenant, there is the corporate people of God, there is God's faithfulness to Israel, there is holiness, and there is mission and calling. I was called to remind people that the salvation of God was for a people, through a people. I reminded people that God's salvation is not centrally about us, rather, it is centrally about him and his plan to redeem all of the creation.

As the feedback from this sort of teaching was generally very positive, I decided to craft my notes into a book. This is that book. Now just for a few comments about the New Perspective.

As one whose theological education and spiritual nourishment is situated within the Wesleyan-holiness heritage, the New Perspective has gained much of my sympathy and all of my respect. This is due in large part to the New Perspective's commitment to practice proper exegesis by giving room to the Scriptures to speak on their own terms. Serious students of the Bible are keenly aware of the risk of interpreting the Scriptures *primarily* in light of our own context; while this is both good and necessary, it must remain secondary to interpreting the text in its own context.

A peripheral goal of this work is to be a Wesleyan voice in the midst of the greater dialogue happening in New Testament studies. During my wonderful periods of research at the Tyndale House, I have quickly and surprisingly realized that one is hard-pressed to find a fellow Wesleyan. It surprises me that within such a rich heritage I only found out about the New Perspective on my own. This means that, at least in my experience, we Wesleyans are not talking much about it, at least as far as I can tell. This is surprising because the New Perspective, just like the Wesleyan-holiness heritage, has quite a lot to say about how to interpret Paul, especially Romans. In particular, we are all quite obsessed with Pauline soteriology. The New Perspective, also like the Wesleyan-holiness heritage, takes up issue with the Reformed interpretation of much of Paul's soteriology. Granted, the New Perspective and the Wesleyan-holiness heritage do not always come out on the same side of the issue, but both do agree the Reformed interpretation needs, well, reformed.

Connected to these is the important reality that there are dividing points within the New Perspective. For instance, Dunn, Sanders, and Wright disagree on a number of items. Being aware of this there is a risk in attempting to represent a school of thought that comprises great internal diversity in a rather generalized way. There is no small amount of controversy surrounding the New Perspective, and N. T. Wright in particular. Nicholas Perrin writes:

> Criticisms of this nature have also been leveled against Tom, but we must be careful. In the first place, it is important to show awareness of the context in which our author speaks. I believe that in future years, when scholars survey his corpus, as they undoubtedly will, they will likely agree that one of the most important theological threads in his writings, not least in his writings on Jesus, is in fact a two-ply cord. This cord involves a commitment not only to challenging what Davies calls the "exaggerated individualisms" among other Gnostic tendencies that today crowd various accounts of Paul and Jesus, but also to offer a compelling apologia—on both a historical and theological level—for a historically rooted and politically relevant Christian faith.[1]

Finally, the goal of this book, once again, is to reexamine the New Testament teaching of salvation and holiness in light of how the New Perspective shines an illuminating spotlight upon the unique context of first-century Judaism in Palestine. The method will be unconventional. The presentation will not be systematic, nor will it be unorganized. We will utilize the indispensable element of the New Perspective's theoretical framework for understanding first-century Palestinian Judaism, the story. Stories are personal. The emphasis of this methodology is to remember precisely that salvation in fresh perspective is something very personal and even more so something very *missional*. That is my intention. I hope that the form reflects the message in a sort of *onomatopoeiatic* fashion. The story is God's story, the great story of God's World Renewal Plan. Read yourself into the story. Become a part of his story, or at least become aware that you are, in fact, a part of the story. It is to the story that we now turn.

Matthew I. Ayars
Cambridge, England, 2015

---

1. Perrin, "Jesus Eschatology," 104.

Acknowledgments

INITIAL THANKS MUST GO to Dr. John Oswalt. Dr. Oswalt's work has been most instrumental in helping me to develop an integrated view of Scripture and holiness doctrine. More than this, I have to thank Dr. Oswalt for his role as a theological reader for the project. I feel as if this work is as much his as it is my own. Finally, I have to thank Dr. Oswalt for his unmatched example of intellectual vigor, strong conviction for the complete message of the Gospel, and academic excellence—truly an inspiration.

After this, special thanks must go to David G. Firth who was graciously supportive of this project even though I worked on it while simultaneously working on my PhD under his supervision. This project undoubtedly prolonged the completion of my dissertation.

Special thanks as well to the Emmaus Biblical Seminary of Haiti family, especially Phil, Emily, Ethan, and Haylie who provide ongoing support with many laughs and sandwiches. You bring life to life.

Finally, to Stacey, Lily, Sofia, and Nora my everything.

Introduction

For too long we have read Scripture with nineteenth-century eyes and six-teenth-century questions. It's time to get back to reading with first-century eyes and twenty-first century questions.

—N. T. WRIGHT[1]

STUDY OF SALVATION

FOR CENTURIES NOW THE judicial metaphor for salvation has occupied center stage of mainstream Christian soteriology. This means that most Christians today define salvation in terms of the substitutionary death of Jesus that offers an escape from the judgment of God by way of grace and forgiveness of sin (atonement) so that when they die they will go to heaven rather than to eternal damnation. This way of thinking about salvation is not wrong, per se, but it is far from complete and even further from a fully integrated biblical soteriology that takes into account more developed and nuanced notions of ecclesiology, Christology, and eschatology. *STUDY OF CHURCH, CHRIST,*

Right away one can identify some issues with thinking about salvation *END TIMES,* strictly in terms of penal substitution. For starters, it is centrally occupied with resolving the sin crisis of the individual as opposed to God and the reestablishment of his reign over the creation. Furthermore, this definition of salvation fails to account for all of Jesus' messianic offices, namely the offices of prophet and king. It also fails to account for Israel's role in the metanarrative of God's *cosmos*-redeeming plan. And what of the covenant? Certainly, the covenant as the pivotal structuring device of Scripture itself must come into play in thinking about salvation, right? And what about the kingdom of God that Jesus was constantly talking about in the gospels,

---

1. Wright, *Justification*, 38.

1

what part does that play in salvation? And holiness? Mission? Pentecost? Where do these pieces fit into the larger picture of Christian salvation?

The point is that the justification and substitutionary atonement-centered soteriology is not the whole story. Mainstream Christianity's thinking about salvation is quite one-dimensional, while Scripture's conceptualization of salvation is as deep, complex and technical as the Bible itself.

So how did we arrive at a place where our soteriology has become so one-dimensional? This way of thinking about salvation finds its origins in Martin Luther's interpretation of Paul's Epistle to the Romans, which more or less launched the Protestant Reformation. Like many interpreters, Luther understood Paul in light of his own socio-religious and historical context, which was mid-to-late fifteenth-century Roman Catholicism. Luther read his own context into the text by assuming that fifteenth century Roman Catholic works-based righteousness was identical to that which the "Judaizers" taught and that Paul so vehemently fought against by espousing justification by grace through faith in Romans and Galatians. Luther took up reading the book of Romans, looking for a way out of his sin-guilt dilemma. Following the Roman Catholic Church's teaching, Luther had done everything in his power to alleviate his sin-guilt by way of good works. However, at the end of the day, the guilt and shame of his sin weighed heavily upon him. In looking for a solution outside of what the Church taught, Luther read the Epistle to the Romans. In reading Romans, Luther learned that his sin-guilt could only be relieved by grace through faith in Jesus Christ thanks to Christ's substitutionary atonement at Calvary. This revelation led to Luther finally receiving the assurance of his salvation and relief from his sin guilt that he longed for. A wonderful story indeed, one that led to the Protestant Reformation, which espoused the authority of Scripture over tradition (*sola scriptura*), and salvation by grace (*sola gratia*) through faith (*sola fide*).

Justification by grace through faith is unquestionably a biblical and orthodox doctrine; however, it is only *one dimension* of a fully developed biblical soteriology. Not only this, but is justification by grace through faith the *thrust* of what Paul was saying, or was Paul actually saying more than this? Furthermore, were the issues that Paul faced in first-century Palestinian Judaism really identical to that which Luther faced in fifteenth-century Roman Catholicism? In other words, what was the context in which Paul was teaching salvation by grace through faith? Perhaps there's more to the story than what Luther was able to see in his time.

Luther's interpretation of Paul is understood today as the "Old Perspective." Its name is derived from its relationship to the "New Perspective of Paul," or simply "New Perspective" (NP hereafter), which we will unpack in just a moment. This Old Perspective of Paul is largely the reason why, when we talk about salvation today as Protestant evangelicals, we talk in large part about justification and the forgiveness of sins. It is our theological and ecclesiological heritage. Over the past few decades, however, the NP has seriously challenged this by suggested a more historically nuanced reading of both Paul and the rest of the New Testament with special emphasis lent to the Gospels.

Interpretive Results of the New Perspective

The NP started as Second Temple Judaism[2] historians challenged Luther's reading of Paul based on the proposition that Luther was reading his own context into Paul, thereby losing sight of some of the more nuanced dimensions of what Paul was saying to his first century audience.[3] Proponents of the NP pointed out that while Paul does indeed teach with certain clarity that salvation can be conceptualized in terms of substitutionary atonement and penal substitution, *biblical soteriology* (i.e., an understanding of salvation that accounts for the entire canon's conceptualization of redemption over and above select readings from the New Testament) is much more historically contextualized and robust than this. When we read Paul on Paul's own terms, as defined by his first-century Jewish context and worldview, we are able to see that Paul's central concern is not substitutionary atonement; rather, his central concern is teaching *how God, in keeping his promises to Israel, successfully completed his plan to redeem the creation from the reign of sin and death through the death and resurrection of Jesus, the Jewish Messiah, and its implications for Gentile believers.* Informing Paul's soteriology was Paul's ecclesiology, eschatology, and Christology, all of which were heavily

2. "Second Temple Judaism" refers to the period of the rebuilding of the temple of Solomon, destroyed by the Babylonians in 586 BC to AD 70 when the temple was destroyed again by the Roman Empire. Also, it is crucial to note that first-century Judaic eschatology was anything but monolithic. However, the community at Qumran, as well as the eschatological posture of believers represented in the Gospels, attests to the fact that the first century was a time of heightened anticipation for the coming of the Messiah. See Chilton and Neusner, *Judaism in the New Testament*.

3. The most notable and prolific NP scholars are N. T. Wright, James D. G. Dunn, and E. P. Sanders.

influenced by his first century Judaic worldview. The NP demonstrates that the apostle was deeply concerned with how the story of Jesus is *continuous* with the story of Israel—something that the Old Perspective fails to engage.

So what are the interpretive results of the NP on constructing a biblical soteriology? More than anything else, the NP seeks to follow the lead of Paul's thinking about salvation in terms of the Old Testament theological heritage. This means that there is first an emphasis on *the role of the covenant* in salvation. Just as in the Old Testament, the covenant is central to God's plan for redemption. It is only the covenant people of God who live under YAHWEH's reign, and only through the covenant and the covenant people that God's redemptive plan reaches the world.

Second, once we properly account for the covenant dimension of salvation, the focus of salvation begins to naturally shift away from the individual and onto the collective people of God.[4]

Third, by thinking in terms of the covenant people of God and the role of Messiah in leading and redeeming his people, the Israel piece falls naturally into place as well. The Messiah is the fulfillment of the righteousness of God to Israel and to the world *through* Israel.

Fourth, the NP reorients us to the central role of the kingdom of God in the Gospel narratives and to the cluster of messianic events (cross, resurrection, and Pentecost) as the pinnacle redemptive event of Scripture. Once again, the concept of kingdom, something that Jesus and the Gospel writers are very preoccupied with, is nearly forgotten in the OP (as well as in mainstream Christianity). More than any other motif, the kingship and messianic identity of Jesus is placed at the center of the message of the four gospels. This naturally challenges the OP's method of building a biblical soteriology solely in terms of Jesus' priestly office (substitutionary atonement).

Marching in step with the NP is an emphasis on the importance of Old Testament theology for Christians. One of the greatest problems of the church today is that it is has inherited a soteriology that is entirely severed from the Old Testament story. We have a tendency to forget that the New Testament solves the problem presented in the Old Testament. The problem of the Old Testament is *not* where people go when they die. Sadly, so much of our twenty-first century thinking has been constructed around

---

4. The implications of this point are far reaching, especially for trinitarian thought and theology, not to mention Christian philosophy at large in terms of ontology and communion.

answering that question and we use passages here and there from the New Testament to support that sort of skewed soteriology. Undoubtedly, the New Testament does answer this question; however, this is a marginal concern at best for the New Testament.

So what is the central question that the Old Testament asks that the New Testament is answering? What is the Old Testament problem that the New Testament solves for us? John Oswalt states it well with this:

> There is one great question that the Old Testament proposes and which the New Testament gloriously answers: "How can a sinful, mortal, finite human being ever live in the presence of, and share the character of, a morally perfect, eternal, infinite God?" That is the overarching question from Genesis to Malachi. The Old Testament does not ask, "How can my sins be forgiven so that I can be assured of going to heaven?"[5]

Salvation in Fresh Perspective: The Goal

So what exactly do I mean by salvation in "fresh perspective"? The NP espouses that fact that Paul himself interpreted the Old Testament in ways never done before, by making Jesus the central point of reference in his interpretive framework and theology. Because of the occurrence of messianic events (cross, resurrection, and Pentecost) Paul was able to approach the Hebrew Scriptures with a completely *fresh perspective*. N. T. Wright highlights the point with this:

> Like many other Jewish thinkers of his and other days, he radically revised and rethought his Jewish tradition (in his case, the viewpoint of a Pharisee) around a fresh understanding of the divine purposes, thus gaining a fresh hermeneutical principle. In other words, I proceed on the assumption that, however we describe what happened to Paul on the road to Damascus ("conversion"? "call"?), its effect was not that he rejected everything about his Jewish life and thought and invented a new scheme, with or without borrowed non-Jewish elements, but that he thought through and transformed his existing Jewish worldview and theology in light of the cataclysmic revelation that the crucified Jesus had been raised from the dead.[6]

---

5. Oswalt, *Exodus*, 4–5.

6. Wright, *Paul and the Faithfulness of God*, 611.

Paul, then, articulated a fresh perspective of salvation to his own socio-historical context of first-century-Palestinian Judaism. It is in this same spirit that this book explores salvation *in fresh perspective* for contemporary mainstream Christianity. The time is ripe to hit the refresh button on how we think about salvation. So much of mainstream Christian soteriology is shaped by contemporary worldview and culture, which is not altogether a bad thing however, as the information and technology age has launched a new moment of evangelicalism in the Western world, it is crucial that we recalibrate our soteriology to account for what the *entire Bible* says about what salvation means for us today. With the proper pieces in place, we will be able to come away with a fresh understanding of salvation beyond me-and-my-sin; a salvation that is centered on the cross as the means for establishing God's reign on earth through his covenant people for all people; a biblical salvation.

The central goal of this book, then, is to offer a "fresh perspective" on salvation by setting a fundamental framework for developing a *biblical soteriology*. The method for achieving this goal, in the same spirit of the NP, is to recalibrate the interpretive lens for reading the New Testament with the two primary points of reference being the theological heritage of the Old Testament paired with the historically nuanced contours of Second Temple Judaism and the first-century Jewish worldview. Special emphasis will be lent to Paul and the thought and theology that frame his soteriology. There will also be a special emphasis on mission and holiness as the ultimate outworking of salvation according to the Christian tradition. *We will see that salvation is ultimately oriented around the faithfulness of God to the creation through Israel in order to reestablish his reign over his covenant people through the Jewish Messiah (Jesus) as his chosen human agent, thereby bringing righteousness back to the created order.*

The Aggregates of Biblical Soteriology: Covenant Cross and Kingdom

So how can we take on such a monumental task in a relatively concise manner? For the sake of accessibility without too much reductionism, I hope to center our approach on the three concepts of *covenant, cross,* and *kingdom.* Acting as the backdrop for these three concepts is the *metanarrative* of Scripture. It cannot be overemphasized that these concepts overlap and flow in and out of one another. I find the metaphor of concrete helpful here. Concrete is made up of aggregates (cement, water, sand, and stone) that when mixed together properly form a single structure. Covenant, cross, and kingdom are the aggregates of biblical soteriology. If we fail to integrate these components, thereby preventing them from gelling, then we will come away with a soteriology that lacks unity. Once again, even though salvation is multidimensional, it is still singular. Salvation is one thing made up of many parts.

Prior to surveying these three aggregates of biblical soteriology, it is crucial that we first consider the role and function of the metanarrative of Scripture. Following that, we will survey each of the aggregates by way of introduction.

Salvation History: The Metanarrative

Salvation is *best* understood when analyzed in its proper context, not when it is extracted from that context and placed on the laboratory table for analysis. In talking about this very issue, Michael Bird writes:

> Beliefs and doctrines are not forged amidst a list of propositions and by logical inferences but in the telling of a story . . . As the old hymn goes, "We have a story to tell the nations," a story that reaches back to Genesis and culminates in Christ handing the kingdom back to the Father: that is the story world of Paul, the story we must grapple with if we are to understand him properly.[7]

The point here is that the Bible is not a systematic theology (neither is Romans).

Salvation, at every point, is framed within a narrative (known as "re-demption history" or "salvation history").[8] The church's pairing of the New Testament with the Hebrew Bible to form the Christian canon is plain attestation from the authoritative Christian tradition that this is how God intends the Scriptures to be read and interpreted. The NP proposes that

7. Bird, *Introducing Paul*, 38–39.

8. Critics of biblical theology propose that the concept of metanarrative is a late one imposed on the Scriptures during the time of the church's forming of the Christian canon. While there is a partial truth to this, there is no doubting that the New Testament writers, Paul and the Evangelists especially, interpreted Jesus in light of the Old Testament narrative. Most importantly, Jesus himself expressed on a number of occasions that he was the fulfillment of the story and promises of the Hebrew Scriptures. This alone provides authoritative precedence for the legitimization of the concept of biblical theology. See Balla, "Challenges to Biblical Theology," 20–27.

Paul understood this. Paul could not think about Jesus in insolation from the Old Testament and the Old Testament in isolation from Jesus. Jesus changed everything about how Paul understood Adam and Eve, the garden, Abraham, Moses, Sinai, the Torah, David, the monarchy, the Prophets (Heb. *Nĕbî'îm*), and the Writings (Heb. *Kĕtûbîm*).

An important part of this is remembering that Paul, being trained as a Pharisee, had a worldview that was shaped by the Old Testament. Paul embraced transcendent monotheism. Paul viewed the world through what he believed to be true about Israel and her patron deity, the single, sovereign Creator of the *cosmos* whose existence was entirely independent from the *cosmos*. This also means that for Paul everything that happened in history hinged on God's great plan to redeem humanity as articulated in the Jewish Scriptures. When Jesus came along Paul didn't just see a God-Man ultimately performing the act of substitutionary atonement, thereby paving a highway to heaven. Rather, when Paul looked upon the life, death, and resurrection of Jesus, he saw a story unfolding *against the backdrop of the greater salvation narrative that began in the Old Testament*. This means that the work of Jesus as the Jewish Messiah was something much more than substitutionary atonement for Paul. This means that the culmination of God's World Renewal Plan was Jesus and his work, his mission to redeem the world that began in the Garden.

What I mean by "God's World Renewal Plan" is God's mission to redeem the fallen, corrupt and decaying creation and to restore things back to the way they were meant to be. This translates into *God's plan to usurp the reign of sin and death over the creation so that his righteous reign through his human agent can be restored*. We will explore this further in chapter 1.

The Covenant

The concepts of covenant and salvation are inseparable in Scripture. We will see that the covenant is *the means through which salvation comes to the world*. Scripture stresses that salvation is *covenant salvation for a covenant people*. Salvation is something that is both collective and individual. At the same time, salvation is not only for God's covenant people, but also *through* God's covenant people. As the chosen people of God take on the loving character of God through being members of the *Messiah-faith covenant people*, their own holiness becomes the fuel for fulfilling the mission of God to the world. In much the same way that holy love drove Jesus to the cross for the salvation of the world, so the holy love of Jesus manifest in the covenant people drives its own cross-bearing mission to continue God's World Renewal Plan—to be ambassadors to the world on behalf of Christ the king. This is the essential core of what we will explore in chapter 2.

The Cross

Normally, in the traditional interpretation of the cross, there is a focus on the cross as substitutionary atonement, or penal substitution (the priestly office of the Messiah). Oftentimes, however, what gets left out are the other messianic offices that are to be interpreted through the cross. We will bring this into perspective by interpreting the cross not only as the moment of substitutionary atonement, but also the moment of Jesus' (ironic) coronation as the messianic king of Israel and the *cosmos*. Special consideration will be given to the cross as the culmination of the mission of God in which the Davidic king fulfills the mission of God by rebelling against the powers of evil (symbolized by a Roman cross) and thereby establishing God's reign on earth. This is the central interpretation of the cross according to the four evangelists. While the evangelists are indeed concerned about the question of substitutionary atonement in the cross, it remains a secondary item for them. Central to the cross is the messianic moment, Jesus as King.

We will see that through the cross and the faithfulness of Jesus, the faithfulness of God manifests *to and for* his covenant people—the faithfulness of God to deal once and for all with the problem of sin and thereby offer an eternal forgiveness, setting right the relationship between broken humanity and the Holy One of Israel. Now that the covenant people are forgiven through Jesus' work on the cross, they are able to be the living, breathing, and mobile tabernacle that bears the saving glory of God to the world. The cross, in other words, is the means by which the mission-centered holiness of God can manifest through the new covenant in the people of God.

Along with this, the cross is the means by which the concept of the people of God moves from being something very *exclusive* to something very *inclusive*. Prior to the cross, it was only the physical family of Abraham that had easy access to the benefits of the promises of God *via* the Torah and Torah observance (obedience to the Mosaic law). The "blessed life," the life "set apart" from the cursed life of the darkened world, was only available to the biological family of Abraham. There is an obvious problem here.

The problem is that God promised that through Abraham *all the families of the world would be blessed*. This had yet to happen prior to Jesus. This means that Israel, because of bearing both the solution *and the problem* to the brokenness of the world, did not fulfill the Abrahamic promise. This is where Jesus and the cross come in. With the death of Jesus, the stipulations of the first covenant are both fulfilled and put to death—forgiveness and justification become available for all people, and the promises of God to Abraham for all the families of the earth are fulfilled *in Jesus the Messiah, who is the embodiment of the true Israel*. With the death of Jesus the curtain that made God's presence exclusive is torn (Mark 15:38). This means not only that through Jesus people can come in but also, through Jesus, the presence of God can go out. This is the core of chapter 3.

Chapter 4 focuses on the dimension of the cross as the second exodus, Jesus as the second Moses, and Pentecost as the second giving of the law code. We will see that Christ was not only a royal figure in the likeness of David, but also a covenant-making figure and liberator in the likeness of Moses. The Scriptures strongly attest to this dimension of Christ's identity and ministry, which we will see. From this angle we are able to see the cross as the means by which the new covenant is made. We have the blood of the covenant shed on the cross that creates a new means through which people can become members of the family of God, or citizens of the kingdom of God, through their faith in Jesus.

The Kingdom

The kingdom of God is the grand finale, the ultimate culmination of the mission of God through the new creation launched in the bodily resurrection of Jesus. God's plan from the beginning was to establish his rule on earth, to establish his theocracy through Jesus. The kingdom launched in the resurrection is the new era; it is the *age of the Spirit*. The old age of the flesh is gone (has been crucified with Christ), and the new has come (has been raised with Christ). God reigns through his people, on earth, *via* the Holy Spirit whom Jesus sends. Because of the many dimensions of this concept, we are at risk of getting too far ahead of ourselves. So let's summarize: holiness is where the love of God reigns on earth through his chosen people, his holy possession, thereby fulfilling his World Renewal Plan.

Conclusion

So, with this, we have a 35,000-foot view of an integrated biblical soteriology. When we place Jesus and God's World Renewal Plan at the center of our thinking about salvation, our soteriology begins to line up quite well with the Bible's conceptualizations of what it means to be saved. With this, the goal is *not* to move *away from* substitutionary atonement as a crucial dimension of Christian doctrine; rather, the goal is to properly situate substitutionary atonement in its appropriate context as a piece of a much larger image that is God's World Renewal Plan.

Part 1

God's World Renewal Plan

---------- 1 ----------

The Salvation Narrative

God's Story

The treatment of salvation in Exodus is all the more powerful because it is told in the context of narrative. Mahatma Gandhi reportedly told his friend, American missionary E. Stanley Jones, that he did not believe the Bible was divine because it was composed largely of stories. Apparently, he thought that divine revelation should take the form of bare, contextless pronouncements, as the Koran or many of the Hindu books do. But we believe the Bible is divinely inspired, not in spite of large sections in narrative form, but precisely because it appears in such a form.

—JOHN OSWALT[1]

I RECENTLY ENCOUNTERED A well-intentioned Christian brother sporting a bright orange T-shirt. The shirt had a graphic borrowed from the popular board game Monopoly. The graphic was a Chance card that said in bold font, "Get Out of Hell Free." This, for far too many Christians, sums up Jesus, the cross, and the resurrection. Believe in Jesus and you'll be issued a "Get Out of Hell Free" card. Really? Is it really that one-dimensional? Does this sum up the sixty-six books of Scripture, the promises to Abraham, Israel, David, the disciples and the church today? Is this what it's all about?

To borrow the phrase that Paul repeats again and again in Romans, "By no means!" (Rom 3:4, 6, 3; 6:2, 15; 7:7, 13; 9:14; 11:1, 11). How have we

1. Oswalt, *Exodus*, 6.

15

ended up in a place where our theology warrants propagating the Gospel of Jesus Christ as being synonymous with a "Get Out of Hell Free" card? I'm sure the answers are many, but the bottom line, I believe, is that we have tragically lost sight of the salvation narrative. This is what Sandra Richter means when she says, "most Christians have not been taught that the story of the Old Testament is their story . . . The church does not know who she is, because she does not know who she was."[2] Thankfully, Paul did not make this mistake. It is when we read Paul (as well as the entire New Testament) without the Old Testament in sight that we end up with bad theology T-shirts (and bumper stickers).

The church must remember who she was. This means recognizing that salvation is not centrally about me-and-my-sin-crisis, it is about Jesus and God's World Renewal Plan. N. T. Wright says, "The theological equivalent of supposing that the sun goes round the earth is the belief that the whole of Christian truth is all about me and my salvation."[3] We have to remember that the New Testament authors were interpreters of the Old Testament and understood their stories to be intimately connected with that of the Old Testament.

Not only must we have knowledge of the characters, events, and places of the Old Testament, but we must also have an integrated view of the Old Testament, its message and its theology. We must be able to go beyond knowledge of what the Old Testament says to arrive at a place where we know what the Old Testament *means*. We must broaden our lens so as to see the whole picture of the Old Testament in order to understand how the New Testament links up with it, and how the history of God carrying out his single plan to redeem creation takes shape throughout.

We get into interpretive trouble when we forget that in reading Scripture we are dealing with a single story that runs through all of Scripture. It is when we separate ourselves from this history, from our heritage, that we end up with an understanding of holiness and salvation that knows only of me-and-my-sin-crisis and going to heaven. God forbid!

The gospel, *the full gospel*, is much deeper, richer, and more profound than this. It is about so much more than where we spend life after death— it's about so much more than God alleviating me of my sin-guilt so that I can go on living a happy and peaceful life in communion with God. This is merely a *part* of the story. The full gospel is a complex thing that cannot,

2. Richter, *Epic of Eden*, 17.
3. Wright, *Justification*, 23.

and should not, be flattened out or deflated by removing or neglecting the story of God's faithful plan to redeem all of the creation *through his chosen people.* The full gospel is a far cry from being summarized in a "Get Out of Hell Free" card.

When we lose the complex backdrop of God's World Renewal Plan while reading the New Testament and interpreting God's salvation into our daily lives, it will greatly impact the way we think about salvation. From the perspective of me-and-my-sin-crisis, *salvation becomes something that's primarily about me.* Salvation certainly concerns the individual, but when we read the story of Scripture properly, we begin to see that *my salvation is for a purpose that goes beyond my peace of heart and mind.* We can be moved by the idea of a perfected will and fully devoted heart, *but we must not end there.* God forbid! We will see that salvation, and holiness in particular, is something very missional. When we get this piece right we then begin to move into embracing and understanding the *full gospel.*

So what is the full gospel? The full gospel can only be properly placed in perspective when read as a story. The full gospel is the metanarrative of Scripture. Now we turn to define what we mean by the "metanarrative of Scripture."

Defining Salvation Narrative: God's World Renewal Plan

In a phrase, *the salvation narrative is the story of God's single plan to rescue the creation from the oppression of sin and death by reestablishing his righteous governance (the kingdom of God) over creation through his chosen human agents.* What we are talking about is God's World Renewal Plan—the coming of the kingdom of God on earth as it is in heaven. We are talking about God's plan to rescue the creation from its condemnation, corruption, and decay, which are the consequences of human disobedience and moral autonomy.[4] This Plan is multifaceted, and its various dimensions are integrated and have overlapping layers. We will see this as we progress through God's World Renewal Plan as the crucial framework for understanding salvation.

This single mission to the world through Israel is precisely what shapes New Testament theology. What we're talking about is *monotheistic covenant theology.* The New Testament understands the death and resurrection of the

4. Note to the reader: I will use the phrases "God's World Renewal Plan," "salvation narrative," "metanarrative," and "salvation history" interchangeably.

Messiah strictly through the lens of God's covenant with Israel, reaching clear back to Genesis. The new covenant that is launched with the death and resurrection of Jesus is a *continuation of God's greater Plan*. This is true in much the same way that the Mosaic covenant established at Sinai is *continuation* and fulfillment of the covenant God made with Abraham in Genesis 15. Thinking about Sinai without Abraham would be a mistake. Such a mistake would lead to misinterpreting the theological and historical implications of what happened at Sinai. Moses and Abraham are characters in the same, continuous story. Abraham's story prepares for Moses' story, which prepares for Israel's story, which prepares for Jesus' story, which prepares for the church's story.

Further still, reading the prophets without Sinai in view would be, for the same reason, a major interpretive fallacy. Without being mindful of the covenant and its stipulations established at Sinai, we would be entirely unable to understand the basis of God's judgment and hope pronounced through the prophets.

All this to say that there is only one proper way of framing our thoughts about the kingdom of God and the new covenant that Jesus preached and taught, and that is around God's World Renewal Plan. This is precisely why we can't read Paul without hearing about Abraham, Israel, and even Adam. This is also why we can't read the Gospels without reference to the kingdom, the Messiah (Christ), the Son of Man, and David (we will unpack this further in later chapters).

The idea here is that the Bible is a single salvation narrative of God's World Renewal Plan that begins in Genesis and ends in Revelation. Paul was an excellent interpreter of Scripture because he properly took into account salvation history. As a first-century Jew with a vocation to expand the kingdom among Gentiles, it was the only way he could interpret Jesus, the cross, the resurrection, and Pentecost. Paul's calling to preach the gospel among the Gentiles is seated in the context of the coming of a new age situated in the greater timeline of God's redemptive plan (i.e., Jewish covenant eschatology). This all-encompassing lens is what makes Paul's theology so multifaceted (and often times hard to understand). Paul's thought and theology properly accounted for salvation history, the Roman Empire, the Jews, and most importantly Jesus, as characters in an epic drama that began all the way back in Genesis. Each of these key players had their specific place within the fulfillment of God's promises to Israel and to the world for renewal.

This means that the story of Jesus, the cross, and the resurrection is *not* a new story. N. T. Wright speaks to this by saying:

> The "reinterpretation" or "reworking" in which Paul engaged was seen by him not as a new, quirky or daring thing to do with ancient traditions, but as the true meaning of those ancient traditions, which had either gone unnoticed or been distorted by more recent readings of Israel's Scriptures and the movements of life and culture in which those readings played a key part.[5]

The story of Jesus, the story of Adam and Eve, Abraham, Moses, Israel, David, Nehemiah, and Isaiah the prophet *are all the same story*, and Paul read it that way. He understood salvation and holiness in light of the people, places, and events of the greater story.

As is reflected in bumper-sticker theology, this concept is far removed from the thought life of the average Christian interpreter of Paul. Historically, the church has come away with what seems to be at times a rather obscured interpretation of Paul, or at best, an interpretation of Paul that doesn't seem natural to what Paul may be saying. The serious neglect (and misinterpretations) of Romans 9–11 (and I would even add Romans 7 to this) is proof of this. Perhaps this is why we sometimes struggle so much with some of the passages in Paul's letters.[6] Perhaps we have been reading Paul within an interpretive context that is foreign to Paul's context.

What we need to do is to enter the world of the New Testament. As impossible as this seems, we can at least attempt to do so by taking a step back and describing the greater landscape of the World Renewal Plan as told through the story of Israel, the story of Scripture. We must not, however, describe the story as a fractured story with various chunks that fit together in a cumbersome or haphazard way. We do not wish to simply list the famous characters, places, and events of the Old Testament without taking into account *their connection, their interrelatedness*. We must have an integrated view of both Testaments. Let's turn to that story now with the priority in front of us to understand it as the single story of God's World Renewal Plan.

---

5. Wright, *Paul and the Faithfulness of God*, 46.

6. At the same time we have to remember that Paul was a bit of an enigma to Peter as well (see 2 Pet 3:16). This being the case, we cannot chalk up all of our confusion in reading Paul to ignorance of Paul's worldview. Paul is just plain challenging, which is why we need a fuller, more developed window into the worldview that shaped his theology.

Creation, the Image of God, and God's Reign Over the Creation through His Human Agents

The first chapter of Genesis is one of the most studied passages of the Bible, thanks to contemporary creationism debates.[7] In the midst of those debates we must be careful about how we handle the sacred text of Scripture. It is quite dangerous to force a passage of Scripture to speak to dilemmas that it never intended to solve. The first chapter of Genesis, while certainly inspired *for* a contemporary audience, was not written *to* a contemporary audience. In other words, while Genesis 1 may offer us answers in the midst of a debate about the age of the earth, we can be almost certain that the inspired ancient authors did not have such a debate in mind when writing.

The question we must ask, then, is what *did* they have in mind when writing? What *are* the questions that Genesis 1 is answering? In other words, what is the theological thrust of the creation accounts? Is Genesis 1 really trying to answer a *when* question? Even if it does answer that question, is that the *primary* question it is answering for its readers? I suppose that could be possible. However, it's more likely, as is evidenced by features of the text, that Genesis is much more concerned about *who* than *when*. The theological thrust of Genesis 1, I believe, is not primarily about how old the earth is; it is about who the Creator is.

So, what does Genesis 1 have to say about the Creator and how he relates to his creation? The text makes it clear that the God of the creation is *sovereign*, he is *one*, and he is *good*. These three things do not always go together. Many times, in fact, goodness is absent from power. The rising and falling of human empires throughout the course of human history bears witness to this. Genesis, on the other hand, tells us that God is, yes, a powerful king, *but also a good king*. God is not a dictator. God is, instead, an empowering and freeing God. The jussive verb phrase "let there be" (or some variation of this) appears approximately six times throughout the passage. In order to bring order out of chaos God does *not* issue a series of commands as if he were a hard-nosed monarch forcefully subduing his enemies. God does not use imperative, commanding language; he uses permissive, freedom language. In fact, the only thing that God subdues in creation is the chaos, the darkness.

---

7. For an excellent treatment of this topic see John H. Walton, *The Lost World of Genesis One.*

God uses his power to subdue the crippling chaos so freedom may reign. This is why we witness in the opening scene of the salvation narrative the smooth and formulaic process of God's act in creating: "And God said . . . and it was."

In other words, God's will and capacity to create is *unchallenged*. More than this, he is able to take darkness and watery chaos and effortlessly make order out of it.[8]

God's sovereignty is further accentuated when we compare the creation account with other non-Israelite creation accounts from a similar time and space. The *Enuma Elish*, an ancient Babylonian creation myth dated to the eighteenth to sixteenth centuries BC, is similar to the creation story we find in Genesis. One of the most dramatic differences between Genesis and the *Enuma Elish* (and there are many) is that in the *Enuma Elish*, unlike in Genesis, the physical creation comes about as the result of warring deities. There is a constant *struggle* that goes on between the Mesopotamian gods in the *Enuma Elish*. This is not the case in Genesis. In Genesis, God creates without resistance. In Genesis, God is sovereign and he rules over the creation without resistance and without opposition.

Moreover, in the Genesis account, God is one, not many. There is no pantheon in Genesis. There are no others that can even be compared to YAHWEH Elohim, the God of Israel, the sovereign Creator. The typical elements of the created order that are personified in other ancient Near Eastern creation myths (like celestial bodies) are specifically *not* personified as deities in Genesis. God stands alone on the stage of creation as he peacefully exercises his creative power in bringing life from nothing, light from darkness, order from chaos. There is no struggle or resistance. There is only the God of Israel and his creative will that goes unchallenged.

We also see in the creation accounts that God designed creation in such a way that it requires *governance*. *There is an ordered hierarchy built into creation*. We see this most clearly in God's command to humanity to have dominion over the creation (Gen 1:28). We also see this when God places Adam in the garden and instructs him to "work it and keep it" (Gen 2:15).[9] There are other elements in the creation narrative that point to the reality that the creation needs tending, but we don't have time to detail

---

8. For an excellent literary-theological interpretation of the creation account, see *Epic of Eden* by Sandra Richter.

9. G. K. Beale makes a strong case that in this account in Genesis we see God giving Adam both priestly and kingly roles in working in the garden, which is considered to be the first sanctuary in creation. See Beale, *The Temple and the Church's Mission*, 60–93.

those here. The bottom line is that God creates the *cosmos* in such a way that there is hierarchy, he creates it with a need for rule and governance, *and this is precisely one of the reasons why he creates humanity, to rule over the creation.* Humanity holds a position of authority, a role of governance. He does not intend for humanity to abuse the creation as it sees fit. No, he meant for creation to be managed, to be cared for.

But in what way shall humanity manage it all? They shall manage it according to God's will and *likeness.* The authority of humanity over creation is to be a freeing authority, not a crippling authority, just like God's authority in the creation account. Humanity is not to battle the earth; it is to *enable and free* the creation to be at its best. This concept of freedom-centered, God-like governance is precisely where the role of the *image of God* comes into the story.

With this as the opening scene of the metanarrative of Scripture, we have a clear understanding of how things were intended (by God) to be as exemplified in the peace of the garden of Eden. This is set in opposition to the way things actually are in the actual broken world. In the actual world order must be forced; chaos fights to reign; and darkness, oppression, rebellion, violence, decay, and ultimately death reign. Things are out of order. Things are not functioning the way that God intended. God's plan to rule both *over* and *in* the creation in his goodness through his human agents has been thwarted. The wrong entity reigns over the creation. It is supposed to be humanity who reigns, but humanity's authority to reign has been usurped by the Evil One, by death and destruction.

This establishes for us the backdrop for God's rescue mission. Rather than abandoning the creation because it has run amuck as a result of humanity's self-assigned moral autonomy (which we will explore in detail in a moment), God remains faithful to his plan to have humanity rule over creation in his likeness and thereby set things back into balance (Heb. *šālôm*). We shall see in detail that in order for all of creation to return to peace, a heart change must take place in humanity. *Humanity is the linchpin.* Humanity is the key to God's plan for governance over his good creation. This is a crucial part of where holiness in terms of the *image of God restored in humanity* comes into the picture. This too links up with holiness as mission. We will see that holiness as mission doesn't simply mean holiness as evangelism rather, it means holiness as humanity embracing its *mission to govern the creation according to the love, mercy and grace of YAHWEH himself.*

The image of God in humanity must be restored; it must be regenerated, renewed, put to death and resurrected.

The Image of God: A Vocation

As contemporary readers, we tend to conceptualize the image of God in a way that is quite foreign to the Old Testament and also foreign to Paul's thought. Normally we think of the image of God in humanity as something ontological (having to do with being, or nature). This is certainly true; however, there is another very important dimension to it that cannot go overlooked. This additional dimension comes to light when we interpret the image of God being "built into" humanity in the greater context of the creation narrative. In other words, we must read humanity's image endowment in its respective context of the ordering of creation. This means that the concepts of governance and order in the creation must be accounted for when interpreting what the author of Genesis is telling us when he says that humanity was created in the divine image.

Bearing this in mind, we are able to see that the image of God in humanity is not only about being, it is also about *calling*. This means that the image of God in humanity has two dimensions: (1) an ontological dimension, and (2) a vocational dimension. N. T. Wright brings this back into focus when he says:

> In particular, and following from the vocation of human beings to reflect God's wisdom into the world, this kind of monotheism included the vocation to humans in general to bring God's justice to the world: justice is to human society what flourishing order is to the garden. It was thus, in principle, part of the inner structure of creational monotheism that humans should set up and run structures of governance, making and implementing laws, deciding cases, constantly working to bring a balance in God's world. Human governance was a good thing; it was how the one God intended the world to be run. Human judgment was a good thing, the making of wise and proper decisions about what should and should not be done . . . The word, human life, including ordered human life: all of this was good and God-given.[10]

---

10. Wright, *Paul and the Faithfulness of God*, 628.

So, in the context of the creation and the need for governance, where does the image of God fit in? The image of God is to be the feature of human existence that characterizes the *kind of rule* humanity is to have over the creation, which has been entrusted to humanity by God. In short, *humanity is to reign over the creation in the likeness of God*. Put another way, *human governance is to be marked by self-giving love*. Humanity is to reign the way that God reigns—with mercy, grace, wisdom, and love. With this in place, God, through humanity, maintains his sovereign will in his created world, but *through human agency*. God ensures that his good creation will go on independently under the governance of humanity, but still fulfill its purpose in glorifying him as the good and sovereign Creator. This is the vocational dimension of the image of God.

With this we have the theme of the sovereignty of God running through the creation account start to finish. And what is God's will? His will is for fruitful life and blessing to abound throughout the creation under the watchful care of human beings as the preeminent ones of the created order bearing his image. It is when we arrive in Genesis 3 that things take a wrong turn. Once again, it is only against this background that the reader of scripture can fully understand the World Renewal Plan set in the context of the problem of sin.

Sin and Death Take the Throne of Creation

As we turn to Genesis 3, tragedy enters the narrative. Humanity, rather than ruling according to God's will, decides to do things on their own terms. They abandon God's rule for their own moral autonomy (deciding for themselves that which is good and evil). They wish to live independently from God and free from God's moral norms. This provides for us some background in clarifying why the forbidden tree is called the "tree of knowledge of good and evil" (Gen 2:9). The text reads:

> And the LORD God planted a garden in Eden, in the east, and there he put the man whom he had formed. And out of the ground the LORD God made to spring up every tree that is pleasant to the sigh and good for food. The tree of life was in the midst of the garden, and the tree of the knowledge of good and evil (Gen 2:8–9).

So what does it mean, exactly, that this tree is called "the tree of the knowledge of good and evil"? The serpent offers an interpretation of the tree's title, but his interpretation is *wrong*. We are tempted to default to the serpent's interpretation because it's the only interpretation of the tree's name that we are really (overtly) given.[11] So why is it call the "tree of knowledge of good and evil"? It is because in the act of disobeying God's command, Adam and Eve are *deciding for themselves what is good and evil rather than taking God's word for it* (i.e., moral autonomy). This is moral autonomy: *deciding* for oneself what is good and what is evil. In this sense the serpent is correct in that Adam and Eve have, indeed, become like God in that they have become morally autonomous—deciding for themselves what is right and wrong. *The problem is, however, that this right is reserved for God alone.* God is the only morally autonomous being.

Herein lies the importance of monotheism. With many gods, we have many morally autonomous beings. This means that in a polytheistic setting, morality is relative and moral absolutes are done away with. This is in contrast to the biblical worldview and is strongly rejected by the Old Testament. The existence of absolute morality is possible only with monotheism—one god who decides for all what is good and what is not good.

We see this in the story of the temptation of Adam and Eve. God first declared that it is not good to eat of the tree (Gen 2:17). Genesis then says, "when *the woman saw* that the tree was *good* for food, and that it was a *delight* to the eyes, and that the tree was to be *desired* to make one wise, she took of its fruit and ate, and she also gave some to her husband who was with her, and he ate" (Gen 3:6; emphasis added). We have a problem here. God says it is not good, and Eve sees that it *is* good. She decides on her own, independently from God, what is good. In doing this, Eve does, in fact, become godlike in that she is creating her own moral rules and boundaries. This means that the "knowledge" of good and evil can be interpreted as "deciding for oneself, independent from God, what is good and evil." The consequence is death.

When Adam and Eve disobey God's command, sin and death enter into creation. They chose this even though they are misled into their decision. This is what Paul means when he says in Romans 5:12, "Therefore, just as sin came into the world through one man, and death through sin, and so death spread to all men because all sinned . . ." Now that death has entered the creation through Adam and Eve's willful disobedience, all of the creation is affected by an exposure to corruption and decay. Corruption

---

11. It is common of the Adversary to wrongly interpret the word of God. He does this with Jesus as well in the temptation in the wilderness (Matt 4:1–11).

becomes the governing agent of creation and this translates into a *systemic infection and decay*.

This, by the way, is the essential purpose of Genesis 4–11, to demonstrate that corruption has spread to every inch of the created order. Things are not just a little out of control; things have completely run amuck. It comes to a climax with all of humanity seeking divine status in the story of the Tower of Babel (Gen 11). The creation that God once declared good has been corrupted. Tragically, death and sin through human disobedience have usurped the throne of abundant life.

There are two fascinating points about this. First is that Adam and Eve are deceived into thinking that they can be their own masters and that such a life would be better than being God's subjects. Rather than gaining freedom, however, they become slaves to sin and death. They now have no choice but to die. Such is the nature of existence. Because the originator of all of life is triune, existence is inevitably reciprocally determinant. Being is determined by relationship to one another. Prior to the fall in Genesis 3, human existence was determined by harmonious relationship with the Creator. Now, post-fall, human existence is marked by disobedience and rebellion. No matter how we look at it, our existence is ultimately determined by the nature of our relationship with one another and the Creator. When we lose the Trinity, we loose this critical dimension of the biblical worldview.

Second, and connected to existence and reciprocal determination, is that the sin of an individual always branches out to impact the whole of the individual's network. We see this dynamic throughout the Scriptures. Sin is never something that is individual or static, rather it is always something very communal and organic. We will see later on that this is precisely why holiness is never simply individual, but something rather collective and communal.

Another important dynamic in this story is that these events make it apparent that God, as a part of his design, has created things in such a way so as to allow human decisions to play a role in determining the shape of historyand outcome of events. It certainly was not God's desire for sin and death reign over the creation. He allowed this *cosmos*-changing consequence to come about by means of human choice. After all, what good is a command not to eat of the forbidden fruit if there's no choice in the matter? The command itself presupposes that God has designed things so that human decision can change the course of events. This attest to the fact that the Old Testament rejects the concept of fate or destiny. This is key for the efficacy of the work of Christ. This means that God forfeits dimensions of his sovereignty for the sake of human well-being.

This is very different from the fatalistic thinking that characterizes the thought of the Western world more and more. This dynamic of human free will is crucial in understanding the salvation narrative and God's World Renewal Plan. *The very humanness of Jesus himself as well as his faithfulness as the effective culmination of God's World Renewal Plan hinges on this.* This means that salvation depends on human free will. We will see that if Jesus was forced to the cross and did not go willingly, everything falls apart. Not only is this the case with Jesus, but with believers and holiness, as we will see. It is important that this stays in front of us as we observe the outworking of God's World Renewal Plan.

Even with humanity's failure to rule in God's image, we will find that God is faithful to his original plan. That plan is for humans to be the ones through whom his reign is manifest in the creation.

Abraham and The Chosen Race

So where does the story go from here? How will God's original plan for creation to be run under the stewardship of human agency be restored? If, "The LORD saw that wickedness of man was great in the earth, and that every intention of the thoughts of his heart was only evil continually" (Gen 6:5), what did he have to work with in order to bring things full circle? Thankfully, as we will see, God's plan for salvation depends on his own faithfulness and the *faithfulness of Jesus.*

Before the foundation of the world, God *chose,* or elected, to execute his World Renewal Plan through a single family, the family of Abraham. Through Abraham, God's World Renewal Plan would be accomplished (Eph 1:3–6). Herein lays the proper, biblical doctrine of election and predestination. So many get it wrong, unfortunately. The familiarity with Calvin's doctrine of election and predestation (that he inherited from Luther and that Luther inherited from Augustine) tempts us to think that it is synonymous with the biblical doctrine of election. This is not the case. The biblical concept of election as pertains to salvation is about a corporate, collective people, not individuals.

Let us first explain what the biblical doctrine of election is not. The biblical doctrine of election is *not* that God predetermines who does and who does not go to heaven. *Election according to Scripture is not about God predetermining where individuals spend the afterlife.* This is not a priority concern whatsoever in Scripture.[12] Scripture, especially the Old Testament and Paul (as we will see, Paul is right in step with the Old Testament), is much more concerned with the fact that God *predestined that through the family of Abraham his plan would be fulfilled. Christ is the chosen one through whom people can choose to be a part of God's covenant people by faith.* Paul and the Old Testament teach us, "God's people is a chosen race (1 Pet 2:9), that is, a chosen *group* and not chosen individuals."[13] God chose Abraham and his family. God chose Christ and his church. Everett Ferguson further explains this idea with this:

> All who are in Christ are included in his election. God chose Abraham (and all in him); God chose Jacob (and all in him); God chose David (and his descendants); God chose Christ (and all in him). Just as all who were "in" Abraham, Israel, or David were included in their election, so it is with Christ. The election of Christ entails the election of those in Christ. The plan of God for Christians is spoken of in the same way as for Christ: foreknown (1 Pet 1:20; Rom 8:29), predestined (Acts 4:28; Eph 1:5; Rom 8:29–30), and loved before the foundation of the world (John 17:24; Eph. 1:4). God continues to choose a category, a group—believers in Christ. Christians are in Christ as Jews are in Abraham and humanity is in Adam (cf. Eph 1:10).[14]

This means that God chose, in advance, to overthrow the reign of sin and death through Jesus. Said another way, Jesus was the "elect" one through whom people would be saved. There are God's people and there are those who are not God's people. Individuals have the opportunity to choose to participate, or not to participate, as members of this corporate people of God. This is entirely different than God predetermining where people will spend eternity after they die.

Moving forward from here, we read of God's promise to Abraham in several passages in Genesis. One of the common themes that we read in these promises is that God will turn Abraham's family into a nation, a chosen race, through whom God will rescue the creation from the oppression

---

12. For a more thorough treatment of a biblical doctrine of life after death, see Wright, *Surprised by Hope.*

13. Ferguson, *The Church of Christ*, Kindle location 1109–10.

14. Ibid, Kindle location 156–59.

of sin and death. Through Israel, God will establish his reign on earth. This is precisely what God promised to Abraham in Genesis 22:17–18 when he says to Abraham,

> I will surely bless you, and I will surely multiply your offspring as the stars of heaven and as the sand that is on the seashore. And your offspring shall possess the gate of his enemies, and in your offspring shall all the nations of the earth be blessed, because you have obeyed my voice.

Included in this promise is that God's rule would return to all of creation, to all the nations of the earth, *through Abraham's family*. That reign, however, would depend on the obedience and cooperation of Abraham's family's—it would depend *on faith*.

Ah ha! Once again, here we encounter the dynamic of human will and participation as essential to the plan. Again, we will see the importance of this when we arrive at the faithfulness of Jesus through the cross in subsequent chapters. God's presence among them was dependent on their obedience; it was dependent on their faith, just as it was in the garden of Eden with Adam and Eve. A new order had to be established—an order in which humanity would not submit to the rebellious desire for moral autonomy.

Summary

So when we step back and view the big picture from this point in the story, what do we see? First, we said that it was God's plan for humanity to rule over the creation according to the divine image. After this, humanity rebelled, and sin and death took the throne of creation. Paul encapsulates this reality with the single phrase, "for all have sinned and fall short of the glory of God" (Rom 3:23). At this point, God launched his mission to rescue and restore creation as it was intended to be by staying faithful to his plan to have humanity rule over the creation. God's faithfulness is manifest in his choice of Abraham and his family as the means through which the World Renewal Plan would be fulfilled.

Abraham: The Father of Faith

It is evident right away that Abraham and his family are not without problems. God clearly didn't choose them because of their performance;

he chose Abraham because of his faith (Gen 15:6). Faith in God's promise is, after all, at the center of the patriarchal narrative. We learned from the creation account that God is sovereign. His sovereignty not only serves the purpose of creation, but also serves the purpose of *redemption*. God can bring order out of cosmic chaos as well out of human chaos. *Abraham exemplifies the fact that human faith in, and human faithfulness to, God's ability to transform is an essential element in God's World Renewal Plan.*

One of the problems highlighted in the story of Abraham's family is that Abraham and his wife Sarah cannot have children. In an ancient Near Eastern patriarchal culture, progeny is everything. The capacity to have children means that the name of the family will go on; if this is taken away then the family becomes extinct. For ancient cultures, the continuation of life was of highest priority. John Oswalt points out that Abraham's inability to have children perfectly exemplifies the human problem: death.[15]

God responds to Abraham and his family, who face imminent death and extinction, with a promise:

> Now the LORD said to Abram, "Go from your country and your kindred and your father's house to the land that I will show you. And I will make of you a great nation, and I will bless you and make your name great, so that you will be a blessing. I will bless those who bless you, and him who dishonors you I will curse, and in you all the families of the earth shall be blessed" (Gen 12:1–3).

Not only does God promise Abraham children, but a *nation*. Later on in the story God expands the promise with this:

> After these things the word of the LORD came to Abram in a vision: "Fear not, Abram, I am your shield; your reward shall be very great." But Abram said, "O LORD GOD, what will you give me, for I continue childless, and the heir of my house is Eliezer of Damascus?" And Abram said, "Behold, you have given me no offspring, and a member of my household will be my heir." And behold, the word of the LORD came to him: "This man shall not be your heir; your very own son shall be your heir." And he brought him outside and said, "Look toward heaven, and number the stars, if you are able to number them." Then he said to him, "So shall your offspring be." And he believed the LORD, and he counted it to him as righteousness (Gen 15:1–6).

15. Oswalt, *Called to Be Holy*, 1999.

There are many things happening in this passage and we cannot comment on them all. There are a few elements in this narrative, however, that we cannot afford to miss. First, God does not fulfill the promise right away. Abraham isn't only aware of this, but complains about it to God. *There is a process of building faith; there is a process of growing in relationship.* We will flesh this concept out of the process of faith in later chapters (especially in chapter 5).

Second, in this passage, God's initial promise that we saw in Genesis 12 is expanded with this promise. Not only will God make Abraham a nation, but so much so that his descendants will be beyond enumeration. In addition, this will be a *naturally born* family, not a family from the seed of Abraham's servant Eliezer of Damascus. When Abraham heard God's initial promise, he was thinking that it would be fulfilled by human means (surrogacy).[16] To this God says, "no." Rather, God will break into the brokenness, corruption and decay of the *cosmos* (exemplified by sterility in this case) and regenerate order; he will heal, he will set right that which has gone wrong because of sin. All of this depends, however, on human faith and human faithfulness.

As we progress through the patriarchal narrative, we quickly see that there are moments of great faith, but there are more moments of frustration and brokenness. The very children that God miraculously brings into the world, namely Isaac and Jacob, are a mess! Isaac and his wife, we learn, are sterile as well. God, once again, steps into the picture and regenerates life where there is death. Jacob, Isaac's son and Abraham's grandson, is a master manipulator. Jacob's story comes to a head when he actually wrestles with God himself. (Gen 32:22–32). Even worse than this, Jacob's sons sell their brother Joseph into slavery. All of this from the chosen family, the ones through whom God's redemption will reach out into the world for the sake of regeneration.

All of these testimonies (and there are more) exhibit the great struggle within the chosen family. This means that in the family, the chosen race is God's solution, as well as humanity's problem. We will later see how Jesus, on the cross, exemplifies this once again, but in a new light.

So what do the patriarchal narratives contribute to God's World Renewal Plan? What's the function of this part of the metanarrative of Scripture? The role of the patriarchal narratives in God's World Renewal Plan is

---

16. We see this expectation manifest again in the Hagar and Ishmael narratives in Genesis 16.

that *they are the promise bearers*. They have received the promise from God that through them he will fulfill his World Renewal Plan. Along with this, they exemplify, in a single family, in a single race, the problem of humanity and what it looks like when God engages in his act of redemption with broken humanity. More specifically, the stories of Abraham, Isaac, Jacob, and Joseph *demonstrate the role and function of human faith and faithfulness in response to God's redemptive promises to a broken world.*

Lastly, and most importantly, the patriarchal narratives demonstrate the seriousness of the faithfulness of God. Even with the family's repeated failures, God sticks to his plan and remains faithful to his promise. That promise, however, is dependent on human faith. God's grace is so much more than his wrath. This is partially what Paul means when he says,

> That is why it depends on faith, in order that the promise may rest on grace and be guaranteed to all his offspring—not only to the adherent of the law but also to the one who shares the faith of Abraham, who is the father of us all, as it is written, "I have made you the father of many nations"—in the presence of the God in whom he believed, who gives life to the dead and calls into existence the things that do not exist. In hope he believed against hope, that he should become the father of many nations, as he had been told, "So shall your offspring be." He did not weaken in faith when he considered his own body, which was as good as dead (since he was about a hundred years old), or when he considered the barrenness of Sarah's womb. No unbelief made him waver concerning the promise of God, but he grew strong in his faith as he gave glory to God, fully convinced that God was able to do what he had promised. That is why his faith was "counted to him as righteousness" (Rom 4:16–22).

The Exodus and Desert Wanderings

The exodus is the most important redemptive event in the Old Testament. The exodus is to the first covenant what the messianic events of the cross, resurrection, and Pentecost are to the new covenant. For this reason we will treat in great detail the role and function of not only the exodus and desert wanderings but also the law of Moses in chapter 2. Let us use our time here, as we simply survey the landscape of the metanarrative, to prepare for that chapter.

With Joseph's generation, the sons of Israel (Jacob) are in Egypt because of a famine in the land that God promised them. They go to Egypt for provision. Interesting, isn't it, that what seems like a way out of a bind turns into full-blown slavery a little further down the road?

After ten generations the Israelites have grown beyond a family and into a race. This part of God's promise to Abraham had been fulfilled; what is missing is the land. God not only promised progeny, but also a land in which that progeny would live with God as their sovereign, patron deity. Israel, however, were slaves in Egypt.

The promise of land connects God's World Renewal Plan for a new creation all the way back to the Old Testament. God is not only concerned with redeeming the spiritual; he's concerned with redeeming *all of his creation, including physical dimensions. God continually makes earth a dwelling place not only for his people, but for himself to share with his people as well.* This is Canaan. This is the temple. This is the new heavens and the new earth of Revelation—this is the new Jerusalem.

We have the tendency to think that we were created for *heaven.* This isn't the case. Humanity is created for earth and heaven is to come down and dwell amongst us. The temple is not so much the door to heaven; it is the place where heaven and earth *meet.*

God, in response to Israel's cry for help (Exod 2:23–25), sends Moses as both deliverer and covenant-maker. Moses arrives in Egypt (after being absent from Egypt for a number of years), appears before Pharaoh, and makes a plea to Pharaoh to let Israel, God's people, go. Pharaoh refuses to let Israel go. In response, God sends plagues. The ten plagues that ensue serve to demonstrate the power and sovereignty of God not only over Pharaoh, but also over deified nature. This God of Israel and Moses is the King (capital K), he is the sovereign Creator, and Pharaoh has his people. As the Creator, he maintains his power and authority over the creation, which has fallen out of the authority of humanity and into the authority of depravation, sin, and death.

Let us state briefly that with this we can begin to see that the exodus is a *type* of the messianic events that occur in the Gospels. What (start of sentence) happened with the plagues and Pharaoh in the exodus account points to and parallels the cross in particular. In the exodus, the Pharaoh, who personifies the reign of human arrogance (i.e., moral autonomy), sin, death, decay, and corruption on earth holds God's people captive as his slaves. In the cross, sin and death reign (the human political leader of Jesus' time is Caesar) and hold God's people captive as slaves. In the exodus, God demonstrates his sovereign reign over the creation, even over sin and death, through public demonstration of control over nature and thereby frees his people from their slavery. In the cross, in much the same way that he makes a mockery of Pharaoh and the Egyptian deities, God disarms sin and death by hanging on a cross and walking out of the grave after three days dead (Col 2:15).

With the resurrection of Jesus, we have the public demonstration of God's sovereignty to reign not only over creation, sin, death, corruption, and decay, but also to *free his people from their grip and reestablish their authority over the creation as was originally intended.* We will deal in detail with the exodus as a type of the cross, resurrection and Pentecost in chapter 4.

A feature of this that we cannot miss is that God's redemptive activity in the life of Israel is the result of his *promise to Abraham.* Not only that, but God doesn't simply deliver Israel from Egypt because of their cry. This is only a part of it. He delivers Israel because he promised Abraham a land of his own, a land in which the people of God would dwell in fellowship with their patron deity—a place to walk with God just as Abraham, Isaac, and Jacob did—just like Adam and Eve did. God is keeping his promise to Abraham and keeping that promise means exercising his divine sovereignty to not only exercise control over nature, but also to redeem Israel from their affliction.

Once out of Egypt, God leads Israel on their way to inherit the Promised Land. The geography of the area demanded that this meant passing through the desert—uninhabited wilderness containing nothing on which to naturally live. During their time in the desert, God creates a covenant, through Moses as an intermediary, with the people of Israel just as he did with the patriarchs. There are always stipulations for participating in the redemptive work of God. We will deal in detail with the Mosaic law and its role in the World Renewal Plan in the next chapter.

After receiving the law of Moses as the stipulations for covenant between God and Israel, they move on through the desert, making their way to the promised land. This is a tough time for Israel. Israel proves to be a stubborn and rebellious people, Jacob in particular. Who does this sound like? If God could work his redemptive plan through this rebellious bunch, then he can work with *anyone.* There is hope for all because of the faithfulness of God.

Eventually, Israel arrives on the banks of the Jordan, ready to settle in the promised land; however, there is a problem. There are already inhabitants living in Canaan who claim that the land is theirs! We are already beginning to see that the story of Israel is a continual battle. Step by step, Israel faces challenges to receiving God's promises. First Pharaoh, then the Red Sea, and then the wilderness, now the inhabitants of Canaan. They must not only settle in the land, but they have to colonize it first. If depending on God to survive in the desert for forty years weren't enough of a lesson in faith, then a nation of slaves knowing nothing about warfare going to battle with numerous ethnic groups experienced in battle would surely do it!

We can quickly see the crucial role of human faith in God's World Renewal Plan up to this point in the story. Faith was the subject matter in the patriarchal stories, and here, once again, in the story of the exodus and desert wanderings, we have faith as the focus, and not only faith, but faithfulness also. This is true even of Moses, the deliverer and covenant-maker. Moses, *like Abraham*, at the start of his story depends on his own facility to rescue his own people (with Abraham this is exemplified in the story of Hagar and Ishmael).

Do you remember the story of Moses killing the Egyptian in defense of his people? Moses fails miserably. Moses ends up fleeing from Egypt and wandering in the desert as a shepherd with no homeland. One would think that Moses would have been more effective as a deliverer when he sat on the royal throne of Egypt. This is not the case. *It is when Moses gets off his throne and ends up wandering in the desert as a shepherd that he becomes useful to God.* It is once Moses gets out of the way that God does the true redeeming work.

When God initially calls Moses, he has little faith. Just like in the story of his killing the Egyptian in defense of the Israelite slave, Moses is thinking entirely about *himself*. "But behold, they will not believe me, or listen to my voice . . ." (Exod 4:1). For Moses to be an agent of redemption in God's plan, just like Abraham, he had to get his mind off of himself and on God—he had to have faith.

Moses, then, is a type of Israel. Both need a great deal of faith to respond to the call and promise of God.

Following the death of Moses in the desert, Israel colonizes Canaan and settles there under the leadership of Joshua; in Canaan, they set up a government structured as a tribal confederation, which quickly takes a turn for the worst.

The Tragedy of Israel

Sadly, things do not go well from here. The epic of Israel as recorded in Scripture (and in extrabiblical sources as well) is a tragedy. Abraham's family ended up being a rebellious people just like the rest of humanity. Just like Adam and Eve, Israel failed to obey God's commands as detailed in the Sinai covenant. As a result, the presence, blessing, and glory of God that were intended to spread into the creation through Israel were thwarted once again because of human moral autonomy—because of human pride. This is the story of the bulk of the Old Testament.

It is in the historical books (Joshua—Esther) that we read the details of the tragedy. There are certainly moments of victory, but most of the developments and pivots in Israel's story are, sadly, defeats. The book of Judges depicts a tribal confederation that all but falls apart, with an entire tribe (Benjamin) being nearly annihilated by the other tribes. The books of Samuel and Kings recount the events of the monarchy (both united and divided). While there are a few good kings, most are disobedient.

Just to get an idea, there were forty-four kings total between the united and divided monarchies. There are only eight, yes eight, of these that were said to have been "good" (Asa, Jehoshaphat, Joash, Amaziah, Uzziah, Jotham, Hezekiah, and Josiah). That's an *eighteen percent* success rate. But even with the good kings, just about all of them failed to "take down the high places." What does this mean exactly? In the Torah it is mandated that there should be only one place of worship. This is to represent the singularity, the oneness of the God of Israel.

The Israelites, as far as history tells us, were the first monotheists. Their monotheism was set in strong contrast to the culture of polytheism in the ancient Near East. The patron deity of Israel, YAHWEH *Elohim*, was adamant in revealing to Israel that he was not like the gods of Israel's neighbors in that he was *one*. In fact, the oneness of God is arguably the most important divine attribute revealed in the Torah, and arguably even the entire Old Testament (Deut 6:4). This was to be the testimony of Israel. Again, this was to be reflected in the central place of worship for Israel.

This is critical. For Israel to have more than one place of worship is to ruin their testimony as the chosen race of the One True God. *This is precisely why getting rid of the high places was so important.* To keep the high places was to testify that the God of Israel wasn't sufficient to bring life.

Note here the *missional* dimension of the Mosaic law. God is adamant about the law of Moses *because it is the testimony of the covenant people of*

God to a lost, world. When the law is lost, the testimony is lost with it. This means that when the church loses holiness, it also loses its witness.

So the story of the kings of Israel, like the stories of the judges, like the story of the desert wanderings, like the stories of the patriarchs, is a *tragedy.* Funny, isn't it, that the theme of tragedy runs all the way through the Scriptures. Even to the culminating event of the story when the Innocent One is crucified as a criminal. God redeems it all.

There is one high point, however, in the midst of tragedy that is crucial in the salvation narrative and that is the Davidic kingship. We will touch on the role of the Davidic kingship and messianic promise within the greater scope of God's World Renewal Plan in just a moment.

Exile: The Loss of Faith and the Loss of the Inheritance

The book of Deuteronomy outlined for Israel that if they were not faithful in obeying the Torah then God's presence would depart from the Temple and Israel would be left to face the threat of their enemies on their own. It also made clear that the Promised Land was not Israel's land, but God's land, and that the inhabitation of that land depended on their faithfulness to God through Torah obedience.

To put this in context, we must keep in mind that God was all Israel had. Their covenant relationship with Yahweh Elohim was nation defining. Without the covenant, Israel was merely a nation of slaves. Even more than this, without the heritage of their Abrahamic covenant, their existence would not be possible as God created Isaac in the midst of Abraham's and Sarah's sterility.

We must remember, once again, that Israel came from a promise. Their lack of faithfulness in response to God's promise was the same as Abraham's: curse (Abraham's curse of sterility). In the same way that it was Abraham's faith in God's promise that meant the fulfillment of God's promises and the birth of Isaac, it is Israel's faith in God's promise that activates their eligibility to receive their inheritance as children of Abraham—the inheritance that is the Promised Land.

This meant that God's absence meant vulnerability to an increasingly hostile environment and surrounding nations. When the pressure was on, Israel's faith in God was tested. Israel's repeated failure meant not only vulnerability in the face of their enemies—it also meant that the loss of their land and return to slavery was inevitable. Here's a portion of what we find in Deuteronomy:

> "But if you will not obey the voice of the Lord your God or be careful to do all his commandments and his statutes that I command you today, then all these curses shall come upon you and overtake you. Cursed shall you be in the city, and cursed shall you be in the field. Cursed shall be your basket and your kneading bowl. Cursed shall be the fruit of your womb and the fruit of your ground, the increase of your herds and the young of your flock. Cursed shall you be when you come in, and cursed shall you be when you go out.
>
> "The Lord will send on you curses, confusion, and frustration in all that you undertake to do, until you are destroyed and perish quickly on account of the evil of your deeds, because you have forsaken me. The Lord will make the pestilence stick to you until he has consumed you off the land that you are entering to take possession of it. The Lord will strike you with wasting disease and with fever, inflammation and fiery heat, and with drought and with blight and with mildew. They shall pursue you until you perish. And the heavens over your head shall be bronze, and the earth under you shall be iron. The Lord will make the rain of your land powder. From heaven dust shall come down on you until you are destroyed.
>
> "The Lord will cause you to be defeated before your enemies. You shall go out one way against them and flee seven ways before them. And you shall be a horror to all the kingdoms of the earth. And your dead body shall be food for all birds of the air and for the beasts of the earth, and there shall be no one to frighten them away. The Lord will strike you with the boils of Egypt, and with tumors and scabs and itch, of which you cannot be healed. The Lord will strike you with madness and blindness and confusion of mind, and you shall grope at noonday, as the blind grope in darkness, and you shall not prosper in your ways. And you shall be only oppressed and robbed continually, and there shall be no one to help you (Deut 28:15–29)

With this, God makes it clear to Israel that their disobedience would result in consequences. This highlights the importance of God's mission to redeem the nations through Israel. So important, in fact, that he gives up his very Son to suffer the curse of Israel so that his World Renewal Plan can still be accomplished through his chosen human agent.

Israel was to be a microcosm of the world as God intended it. It was to be God's kingdom on earth. This was the whole point of the Mosaic law. The law was a covenant that outlined the stipulations for a kingdom nation and life. Disobedience to the law meant the death of the testimony of the kingdom of heaven on earth and the failure of the World Renewal Plan, which depended upon human obedience.

God specifies that Israel will be taken over by their enemies—and this is precisely what happens. The people of Israel (and Judah as well) end up in Assyrian and Babylonian exile and lose God's land to pagan nations. The land was a gift—an inheritance. This was true of Abraham in that the fulfillment of the promise was contingent upon *faith*. Israel, because of their lack of faith, loses their eligibility to receive their inheritance, the Abrahamic, redemptive promises of God. Because of their disobedience, they return to the state of slavery, ending up in exile. Yet, even in the midst of the faithlessness of Israel, God remains faithful to his to World Renewal Plan. He is still fixed on making his kingdom come.

The Davidic Kingship:
Your Throne Shall Be Established Forever

God advances his plan to fulfill his promise to Abraham through David. It is in the midst of the tragedy of Israel that we find the story of David. The story of King David is a bright spot in the darkness. David, like Abraham and Moses, demonstrates great *faith*. With this we see the continued development of the role of faith and faithfulness among human agents and God's use of them in his World Renewal Plan. We cannot overstate this fact: the human heroes of God's World Renewal Plan are those who have *faith*. It is not the individuals who perform and thereby earn God's blessing. No, those who have faith that God will and can do what he says he will do are the ones through whom God's promise is fulfilled and through whom his redemption is brought to the world.

Because of David's faithfulness as king, God makes another promise and another covenant. Once again, this promise is through a person, for a people, just as with Abraham (along with the rest of the patriarchs) and with Moses. God's reward to David for his faithfulness is that a member of David's family will sit on the throne that governs the people of God forever—that the line of David is the chosen family (just like the chosen family of Abraham) through whom God's World Renewal Plan will ultimately come to the world. We can call this the promise of Davidic kingship—the promise that the Messiah, the king who will rule with God's righteousness over God's people, and who will bring righteousness and justice to the fallen world through the special anointing of the Holy Spirit, will be from David's family. This is God's promise to David. Once again, it is David's reward for his faith and faithfulness to Yahweh.

We find the details of the promise in 2 Samuel 7 where we read,

> When your days are fulfilled and you lie down with your fathers, I will raise up your offspring after you, who shall come from your body, and I will establish his kingdom. He shall build a house for my name, and I will establish the throne of his kingdom forever. I will be to him a father, and he shall be to me a son. When he commits iniquity, I will discipline him with the rod of men, with the stripes of the sons of men, but my steadfast love will not depart from him, as I took it from Saul, whom I put away from before you. And your house and your kingdom shall be made sure forever before me. Your throne shall be established forever (2 Sam 7:12–16).

This isn't the only place where we read about the promise of a messiah. The prophets had a great deal to say about thecoming Messiah, especially Isaiah. Isaiah is known as the Prince of the Prophets because we find more messianic promises in his prophecies than any other prophet (among other reasons as well).[17] If you were to go through and read all the messianic prophecies in the book of Isaiah, you would find that almost everyone refers to kingship and governance This dimension of messianism is inherent to the title "messiah."

The Messiah is a savior, but *not primarily in a* "he will save you from your sins" *sense.* The emphasis of messianic redemption lies not on propitiation for sins; it lies in the launching of God's kingdom on earth. We read this in Isaiah:

> For to us a child is born, to us a son is given; and the government shall be upon his shoulder and his name shall be called Wonderful Counselor, Mighty God, Everlasting Father, Prince of Peace. Of the increase of his government and of peace there will be no end, on the throne David and over his kingdom, to establish it and uphold it (Isa 9:6–7).

17. See Oswalt, *Isaiah*, 17.

The clear emphasis of the coming king is *governance*—the establishment of a rule that manifests the righteousness of God. This is describing the coming of the kingdom of heaven through the Davidic king.

Once again, through this brief survey, we can see that the redeemer is not only a lamb, not only a door, but also a *king*. We also see that *kingship*, godly order, and rule are the emphasis of the messianic redemption of God's people along with the creation.

The Promise of a New Covenant

There is another element, however, that plays into the coming of the kingdom and order of God through the Messiah on earth and that is *new covenant*. The Messiah would establish the reign of God through his people on earth to redeem the creation through the cutting of a new covenant. The Messiah was not only a kingdom-establisher, but also a covenant-maker, just like Moses.

We see that the blessing that God's chosen people enjoyed had departed from them and they were sent into exile. Even though they found themselves in exile because of their disobedience, God promised through his prophets that he would continue his World Renewal Plan through them, and that plan would be centered on a new covenant through the Messiah. The Messiah would usher in a new age in which the people of God would live under a new covenant. Under the new covenant, the sign of the people of God would no longer be a mark on the exterior body (circumcision, or the Mosaic law); rather, the sign of the new people would be the *very image of God restored*. This internal transformation would take place through the forgiveness of sins and the gift of the Holy Spirit. Jeremiah prophesied concerning this covenant with these words:

> Behold, the days are coming, declares the LORD, when I will make a new covenant with the house of Israel and the house of Judah, not like the covenant that I made with their fathers on the day when I took them by the hand to bring them out of the land of Egypt, my covenant that they broke, though I was their husband, declares the LORD. For this is the covenant that I will make with the house of Israel after those days, declares the LORD: I will put my law within them, and I will write it on their hearts. And I will be their God, and they shall be my people. And no longer shall each one teach his neighbor and each his brother, saying, "Know the LORD," for they shall know me, from the least of them to the

greatest, declares the LORD. For I will forgive their iniquity and I will remember their sins no more (Jer 31:31–34).

We see here that the Jesus' death and resurrection accomplishes that which the Mosaic law could not. The law, even though it was intended to be the means by which God's reign would be restored to the earth through Israel, was unable to *dethrone death*. Once again, God had had stepped in, and Jesus himself took on the form of man to dethrone death. Now it is through faith in Jesus and his redemptive work for the forgiveness of sins that the reign of God is restored and God's mission is completed. The results of that mission is that believers can "be transformed by the renewal of our minds" (Rom 12:1).

What is crucial in understanding Paul's theology as described above is that even though Jesus successfully reestablished God's reign on earth, the old age is still with us. Both the old age and the new age currently overlap. According to Scripture, it is not until the second coming of Jesus that what is left of the old age will be destroyed and the new age will reign supreme, without resistance, in the new creation. This is yet to come.

This being the case, Christians are called to be set apart in the sense that we are not to give into the present powers of the old age by allowing the power of sin and death reign over our hearts and minds. Christians are to live in the midst of a hostile world with God's love and forgiveness as their central point of reference for regenerated human existence.. Those who are in Christ are to be different from those who have not received the gracious gift of forgiveness through Jesus. We are to be different because we have embraced the forgiveness of God. It is the cross that becomes the central point of reference for all thought and theology for the people of God who live as members of the kingdom that has come, and all the while has yet to come in its fullness.

2

Torah Holiness

The Old Testament Covenant Heritage

> For far too long now Christians have told the story of Jesus as if it hooked
> up not with the story of Israel, but simply with the story of human sin as in
> Genesis 3, skipping over the story of Israel altogether.
>
> —N. T. WRIGHT[1]

IN THE PREVIOUS CHAPTER, we explored the broader, metanarrative of Scripture by hitting the highlights and turning points of the story of the Old Testament. We said that a comprehensive and integrated view of the Old Testament narrative was essential for understanding not only Paul's thought but also how both testaments link together and more specifically, how the New Testament's soteriology flows out of its Old Testament theological heritage. We noted the importance of this as originating in the reality that both Jesus and Paul (along with the other New Testament writers) were Old Testament interpreters, which means that they understood salvation first in Old Testament terms. This means that identifying the complementary relationship of the two covenants is indispensable for understanding salvation in fresh perspective.

In this chapter we will narrow our scope a bit further by exploring how the concept of covenant shapes soteriology. Ultimately, covenant is *the means by which God's Renewal Plan comes to the world*. More specifically,

1. Wright, *How God Became King*, 84.

the cross, resurrection, and Pentecost together are the fulfillment of God's *covenant faithfulness* to Israel that simultaneously redeems both Israel and Gentiles (and the *cosmos*). The NP situates this point against mainstream Protestant evangelical interpreters of Scripture who tend to overlook (or at least misinterpret) the concept of covenant when reading Paul. It is when we have the proper grasp of Paul's thinking about covenant as it relates to salvation that we can arrive at a more profound and historically oriented understanding of holiness and mission as the goal of God's World Renewal Plan.

We will begin exploring these features of Paul's thought by looking very briefly at Paul's use of the term "the righteousness of God" (Gr. *dikaiosynē theou*) in light of God's covenant faithfulness to Israel through the cross. We will then move on to look at the Old Testament concept of covenant in its original ancient Near Eastern context with the specific goal of demonstrating that the purpose of covenant is holiness. Finally, we will consider how the Torah fits into the bigger picture of God's World Renewal Plan.

With these items collectively before us, our goal is to come away with a sharper view of how Paul understood salvation holiness in light of the covenantal framework for salvation. We will see that for Paul, covenant is (1) the means for revealing the holy character of God, (2) the means for revealing the sin problem, (3) the means for solving the sin problem within Israel, and finally (4) the means for solving the sin problem that pervades the *cosmos* In sum, with no covenant, there is no salvation, no holiness and certainly no mission of God.

Creation and Covenant and the Faithfulness of God

So, how does the concept of covenant impact Paul's thinking? According to Paul, redemption comes to the *cosmos* because of God's faithfulness to his covenant with Israel. Without God's covenant faithfulness to Israel, there is no Jesus, there is no cross, there is no resurrection, there is no redemption, and there certainly is no holiness—not for Israel nor the rest of the creation.

This means that God's covenant with Israel is essential. Furthermore, it is essential for Paul that the messianic events of the cross, resurrection, and Pentecost are together the culmination of God's faithfulness to Israel and *simultaneously to the creation at large*. Paul was especially focused on this particular dimension of Christ's redemptive work because he was a

Pharisee ministering to Messiah-believing Gentiles. This means that Paul's mission to the world centered on this idea. Deviation on a single detail of this issue could make or break Paul's ministerial *raison d'être* as an apostle to the Gentiles. This is why Paul was more passionate about this particular point of theology than most others (the strength of language in his epistle to the Galatians alone is proof of this). For Paul, removing the banner of "God's covenant faithfulness to Israel" from above the cross would mean doing away with redemption altogether.

Not only is this issue a hot topic for Paul, but also for the NP. The NP has championed the fact that if we don't get this bit right, the rest will be askew and our thinking about the cross and resurrection will run amuck (which is precisely what it has done in so many cases). But why is the issue so important? How does wrong theology of the cross impact us? For one, it gives us latitude to grossly misinterpret the cross as granting license to sin (*mē genoito!*) as opposed to offering the world the means for a renewed nature. The cross is to be a means by which the sin nature and sinning can be done away with and is not meant to provide justification for an ongoing pattern of sinning.

If we remove the fact that the redemptive work of Jesus is first and foremost the manifestation of God's covenant faithfulness to Israel, then we lose sight of the fact that *the goal of the cross is holiness, which is the embodiment of the image of God in both the individual believer and the collective covenant people of God.*

This is precisely the point that N. T. Wright is making in the quote at the beginning of this chapter. As interpreters of Paul's writing who are far removed from the original context of Paul and his worldview, we have the tendency to emphasize the *Gentile dimension* of Paul's soteriology (solving the Genesis 3 problem) and simultaneously neglecting the Jewish dimension of God's covenant faithfulness to Israel (solving the Israel problem).

The New Perspective on "The Righteousness of God"

The NP has spent much of its efforts resituating what Paul means by *dikaiosynē theou* ("righteousness of God") into this context of God's covenant faithfulness to Israel. We do not have time here to cover the details of the broader discussion concerning what Paul means precisely by "righteousness of God." Michael Bird, however, offers this excellent definition that takes into account the key components of that broader discussion:

The "righteousness of God" is an all-encompassing act that implements the *entire plan of salvation*, including justification, redemption, atonement, forgiveness, membership in the new covenant community, reconciliation, the gift of the Holy Spirit, power for a new obedience, union with Christ, forgiveness of sin, and vindication at the final judgment.[2]

Essentially, the NP has brought into focus the fact that when Paul talks about the righteousness of God (particularly in Romans), he's first talking about his *covenant* faithfulness—that by standing by his promises to Israel he is rightfully fulfilling his part of the covenant with Israel. N. T. Wright says this:

He [Paul] is not simply assuming an implicit narrative about how individual sinners find a right relationship with a holy God (any more than he is simply assuming an implicit narrative about how Gentiles can have easy access to God's people). In so far as he would be happy with the former way of stating matters at all, he would insist on framing it within the much larger question of how the creator God can be true to creation, how the covenant God can be true to the covenant, and how those things are not two but one. And that is what the phrase *dikaiosynē theou* is all about.[3]

But how does the proper, historically oriented interpretation of *dikaiosynē theou* impact Paul's doctrine of holiness? Ultimately, as others have already pointed out (especially John Oswalt),[4] *holiness is the goal of covenant salvation*. As we reorient ourselves to Old Testament covenantal context when interpreting the New Testament (as the NP has done) this becomes much clearer. Leaving out the Old Testament bit, leaving out the Torah bit, leaving out the Israel bit, leads to a gross misinterpretation not only of Paul, but of the entire goal of the cross to begin with.

2. Bird, *Introducing Paul*, 94; italics in the original.

3. Wright, *Paul In Fresh Perspective*, 37. It is also important to note at this point the NP's emphasis on how the concept of covenant dovetails with the apocalyptic for Paul. Cf. Wright, *Paul In Fresh* Perspective, 50–58. While the treatment of the issue is rather complex and highly debated, the NP essentially argues that the launching of a new covenant, made available to both Jews and Gentiles, through the death and resurrection of the Jewish Messiah, was, for Paul, the revelation of the mystery of God right in the middle of the story. This is what Paul is referring to when we talks about the mystery of Christ (Rom 16:25; 1 Cor 4:1; Eph 1:9, 3:4, 6, 9, 5:32, 6:19; Col 1:26, 27, 2:2, 4:3; 1 Tim 3:9).

4. See Oswalt, *Called To Be Holy*.

If the NP is saying, "we must remember that the cross is the manifestation of God's covenant faithfulness to Israel," then I would make the statement more precise by augmenting it to say, "we must remember that the cross is the manifestation of the *Holy One of Israel's* faithfulness to Israel in making them *holy*, in letting *them share his very nature*." In other words, when we leave out the Israel part of the story, we miss out on the very goal of salvation and that is to *provide humanity with a new nature by solving the sin problem*. It is the story of Israel, the story of Sinai, the *covenant itself*, which reveals the need for holiness, the holy character of God, and makes a means for the regeneration of the human sin nature. The bodily resurrection of Jesus is not only the launching of the new creation, but also the launching of a *holy* creation.

To clarify further still, let us specify in what way God's covenant faithfulness to Israel has a dual result. We learned from the previous chapter that there are *two* groups that require God's redemptive work: (1) the nation and family of Israel, and (2) the rest of the creation. Both have their problems, all of which flow from the central issue of the reign of sin and death within the created order.. On the one hand, God made very specific promises to Israel as his covenant people. Included in those promises was the promise that a Hebrew (member of the family of Abraham) would be the righteous ruler and judge of Gentile nations and races. With the death, resurrection, and ascension of Jesus as the Jewish Messiah, *this is precisely what happened*. It is a Jewish man that sits at the right hand of the Father in heaven today and it is that very man who will judge the living and the dead. To this Jewish man all power and authority has been given over the earth and under the earth. This means that God was faithful to this particular promise to Israel.

The second promise that God was faithful to fulfill in the work of Jesus was the promise for a new covenant in which Israel would be liberated from their sin nature (as well as physical exile which embodies the reality of slavery to sin). We read this promise in Jeremiah 31:31–34. Through the death and resurrection of the Messiah all believers have access to baptism in the Holy Spirit, which symbolizes receiving a new nature, a new heart: a heart of flesh. Once again, this promise to Israel is fulfilled in Jesus.

A third promise that we cannot miss is that righteousness would come to the world through Israel as God's covenant people. In chapter 4 we will see in detail how the death of Jesus brings righteousness both to Israel and the world though the fulfillment of the stipulations of the Torah. The point for now, however, is that it is through Jesus that righteousness of heart and life comes to the earth.

A fourth promise that is fulfilled in the cross is the promise to Abraham that all families of the earth would be blessed through him. In Genesis 12:3 we read, "I will bless those who bless you, and him who dishonors you I will curse, and in you all the families of the earth shall be blessed." This fourth promise is the one that leads us into the second dimension of God's covenant faithfulness to Israel. We will see that in just a moment.

With these promises (and there are others), we see that Jesus is the manifestation of God's covenant faithfulness to Israel. This means that through the death and resurrection of Jesus God has acted *rightly* in fulfilling his promises to Israel.

The second dimension of God's covenant faithfulness to Israel is the fact that the rest of the creation (in *addition to* Israel) is also redeemed through Jesus' death, bodily resurrection, and ascension. How does this work? Elohim is not only the patron deity of Israel, he is also the sovereign Creator of the *cosmos*. And the Creator God has rightfully taken on the responsibility to set right what went wrong in Genesis 3. We said in the previous chapter that the problem in Genesis 3 came about as a result of humanity's choice for moral autonomy (embodied in Adam and Eve); corruption, decay, and death entered into God's good creation. To solve that problem God would create again, and that new creation, which will be holy, pure, and marked by righteousness, *will come through the Jews* (connecting back to the promise to Abraham).

Michael Bird helps us with this diagram:[5]

Spheres	Execution	Revelation in the Gospel
Creation	Punitive justice Restoration of creation Reaches the nations	Gift of a righteous status Life and resurrection Rectification of cosmos
Covenant	Faithfulness to the covenant Atonement for sin Devilerance of Israel	Redemption from sin Transformation to new life Membership in the new covenant

When we look at the big picture this way, the story of Israel can be seen as a *story within a story*. Israel's story is embedded in the larger narrative of the fallen creation. Humanity at large, like Israel, cannot live up to

---

5. Bird, *Introducing Paul*, 95.

God's covenant stipulations. This is what we see in Genesis 3 where God very clearly commands Adam and Eve not to eat of the tree, yet they do it anyway. They violate the "Garden of Eden Rules."[6] In much the same way, to resolve the sin problem brought into the world through Adam and Eve's disobedience, God chooses to "adopt" Abraham's family through whom he will execute his World Renewal Plan. What is crucial to note at this point is that Abraham and his family embody both the problem and solution of the *cosmos*. This means that God cannot simply "fix the world" through Abraham's family; he must first fix Abraham's family as well because they themselves, as members of the fallen creation, are subject to the decay of the broken order. They too suffer the same problem we saw in the garden of Eden: *infidelity to the covenant*.

What we see here is that Israel is a microcosm of all of humanity. While there are these similarities, there are also crucial differences. The major difference is that Israel has the Torah, the covenant that details with great specificity with God's expectations for Israel's behavior as his people. We will see how the Torah works itself into this multi-dimensional story in detail in just a moment. The bottom line for now is that through the cross and resurrection, Jesus fulfills the covenant stipulations of both Israel and the greater *cosmos*, thereby liberating not only Israel, *but also the entirety of humanity* through his redemptive work. And this is precisely why "unity in Christ" between Jews and Gentiles is so crucial, even as the Jewish people's uniqueness is maintained (Rom 9–11).

John Oswalt makes the same point with this:

> The need for salvation is a divine/human problem. In short, it is a human problem that creates a divine problem. For the Hebrew people to be in bondage in Egypt was a problem for God, because he had promised to give them the land of Canaan, so he could not leave them there. They were his people, and if he left them in bondage, the whole world would know that YAHWEH was not true to his word. He had to deliver them.
>
> The same thing is true for the whole human race. Our sin with its resulting shame and disaster is a divine problem. God cannot let us go. He cannot sit passively on the sideline, watching the people he made in his own image plunging into eternity without him. So when you feel yourself in the depths, remember that that is God's problem too. When you feel you have failed and wound up

---

6. Sandra Richter (and others, including Beale) has strongly argued for specific covenant language in the garden of Eden narrative of Genesis 3. See Richter, *Epic of Eden*.

in the bondage of guilt and shame, that is God's problem too. The need for salvation is a divine/human problem.[7]

So where do we stand at this point? When we account for the dual dimension of God's faithfulness we can understand with Paul that God takes care of both of these in one fell swoop through the cross. Through Jesus, God's covenant promises to Israel are fulfilled (the establishment of the king of Israel over the *cosmos* and God's sharing of his own holy nature with his people) and the new creation is launched in the resurrection (defeat of death) of Jesus, thereby providing the solution to the *cosmic* problem as well.

At this point let me restate (as it cannot be overemphasized) the fact that if we neglect Israel's part of the story, if we neglect the covenant, we lose altogether what salvation is all about. We lose the need for God's redemption, we lose sight of the need for a new creation, and we lose sight of the nature of God himself. This is precisely where the topic of holiness fits into what the NP has shown us.

Now let's explore how we get from point A to point B on the matter by exploring the Old Testament concept of covenant.

Old Testament Concept of Covenant

In establishing the Old Testament concept of covenant, we will first look at the Hebrew word *bĕrît*. After defining *bĕrît*, we will explore the concept of covenant as being rooted in the ancient Near Eastern patriarchal conceptual framework of fictive kinship. Finally, we will treat the impact of how and why Paul mixes metaphors for salvation.

Defining Bĕrît

The Hebrew word for "covenant" is *bĕrît*. The first time this word appears in the Old Testament is in Genesis 6:18 where God says to Noah, "But I will establish my *covenant* (*bĕrît*) with you, and you shall come into the ark, you, your sons, your wife, and your sons' wives with you" (emphasis added). *Bĕrît* appears another seven times throughout the flood narrative. The context in which the term is used makes it clear that *bĕrît* means "agreement" or "contract."

7. Oswalt, *Exodus*, 121–22.

Inherent to the meaning of "agreement" is the idea that there are responsibilities for both parties to uphold. For Noah, the covenant stipulates that he must be fruitful and multiply and fill the earth (Gen 9:1b, 7), as long as he does not eat meat with the blood still in it (Gen 9:3–4) and does not kill humans (Gen 9:6). In response, God promises "that never again shall all flesh be cut off by the waters of the flood, and never again shall there be a flood to destroy the earth" (Gen 9:11). God then gives the rainbow as a sign to seal the agreement. He says, "This is the sign of the covenant that I have established between me and all the flesh that is on the earth."

The concept of covenant as an *agreement* is not at all foreign to our modern English vocabulary. We can talk about covenants, or contracts between employers and employees (detailed in a work contract). We also talk about treaties or alliances between political parties. While these concepts are familiar, there is a dimension to the Hebrew word *běrît* that is indeed foreign to modern use of the word "covenant." The foreign dimension doesn't appear in the word itself, however; it appears in the verb that's associated with *making a covenant*.

In English, we talk about "making" or "having" a covenant. Hebrew, however, does not conceptualize covenants this way. Hebrew, rather, talks about "cutting" (Heb., *kārat*) or "establishing" (Heb., *qûm*) a covenant. This verb "to cut" is linked to the animal sacrifice that functions as a ceremonial authorization of an ancient Near Eastern covenant.[8] When two parties "cut" a covenant, for whatever reason, whether political, familial, religious, etc., there is an animal sacrifice involved. The two parties would cut the animal in two parts. Killing the animal becomes an outward symbol of the covenant stipulations. More specifically, the sacrifice served to symbolize death as the consequence of violating the covenant. This underlines the *seriousness of the agreement*. The nature of the covenant is *familial*, thus the term "fictive kinship" that we will now explore.

Fictive Kinship

Let us first look at a couple of examples of covenants as fictive kinship in the Old Testament, then, with the illustrations before us, we will define the concept. One of the best Old Testament examples of fictive kinship through cutting a covenant is found in Genesis 15. In this account, God promises his faithfulness to Abraham; he then instructs Abraham to sacrifice a series

---

8. Koehler et al., *Hebrew and Aramaic*, 157.

of (ceremonially clean) animals and separate the halves of the animals' bodies. After Abraham follows these instructions, he falls into a deep sleep. While sleeping he has a vision of God's presence passing between the divided carcasses. The text reads this way:

> When the sun had gone down and it was dark, behold, a smoking fire pot and flaming torch passed between these pieces. On that day the LORD made [Heb. *karat*] a covenant with Abram, saying, "To your offspring I give this land, from the river of Egypt to the great river, the river Euphrates" . . .(Gen 15:17–18)

In passing between the carcasses, *God is sealing his promise to Abraham.* His passing between the carcasses symbolizes that if he does not uphold his promise then he is subject to the punishment of death.

We see this same dynamic at work in Exodus when God establishes his covenant with Israel at he foot of Mount Sinai in Exodus 24. The text reads this way:

> Moses came and told the people all the words of the LORD and all the rules. And all the people answered with one voice and said, "All the words that the LORD has spoken we will do." And Moses wrote down all the words of the LORD. He rose early in the morning and built an altar at the foot of the mountain, and twelve pillars, according to the twelve tribes of Israel. And he sent young men of the people of Israel, who offered burnt offerings and sacrificed peace offerings of oxen to the LORD. *And Moses took half of the blood and put it in basins, and half of the blood he threw against the altar.* Then he took the Book of the Covenant and read it in the hearing of the people. And they said, "All that the LORD has spoken we will do, and we will be obedient." *And Moses took the blood and threw it on the people* and said, "Behold the blood of the covenant that the LORD has made with you in accordance with all these words" (Exod 24:3–8, emphasis added).

Once again, what we have here is a very clear example of what a covenant means in the Old Testament. But how does the dimension of *family* enter into the picture?

The blood sacrifice involved in covenant making is a remnant of the origins of the concept of *fictive kinship* in ancient Near Eastern patriarchal culture.[9] Originally, covenants were to serve as a means for creating *concep-*

---

9. "Ancient" denotes the beginning of recorded human history to the early medieval period (c. fourth century AD). "Near East" denotes roughly western Asia and northeastern Africa.

tual family bonds between parties.[10] Covenants such as these could be an act of marriage or adoption. The blood-sacrifice was to serve the purpose of symbolizing the reality that even though two parties were not of the same bloodline, they would relate to one another as if they were, thereby creating a fictive kinship between them. This is the same idea that is at the heart of a man and woman becoming one flesh in marriage. Though they are not physically born of the same family, they will live with a commitment as if they were.[11] The same principle is true with an adopted child.

Mixing Metaphors: Family and Kingdom

This means that in the symbol of the blood we have a direct, symbolic link to fictive kinship at the core of the concept of covenant. This isn't the only indication, however, that the *nation-identifying* covenant between Israel and YAHWEH as their patron deity goes beyond politics. The Old Testament is filled with familial language to describe the relationship between God and Israel. This means that we have the mixing of metaphors for understanding covenant.[12] On the one hand, we have the political dimension of the covenant that is very present in the story from Sinai.[13] On the other hand, we have the familial dimension that really comes through in the prophetic literature and more importantly, the patriarchal narratives. This reminds us that what is happening at Sinai, while it is indeed a "nation" being established, it is also a *family* that is emerging with its identity in YAHWEH as the figurative patriarch of the family *of Israel*.

We noted before that sterility is a problem among the chosen family. The problem is *not* warring states, or other tribes, or nations threatening a people group. No, the problem is that this family cannot continue on in

---

10. Sandra Richter explores this concept thoroughly in *Epic of Eden: A Christian Entry into the Old Testament*.

11. This concept is made literal through reproduction, of course. This is why the child is the symbol of the unity of man and woman.

12. Historically, this wouldn't be a "mixed metaphor" per se because the origins of government are found in the family structure, then moving into a tribal structure, then national, etc. For the ancients, a "nation" was a "family," so to speak.

13. The Sinai narrative on the creation of the covenant is dominated by Hittite Suzerainty-Vassal Treaty language. This was a type of political treaty of the Hittite empire of the ancient Near East. Once again, even though this is political language, the conceptualization of what's happening with this political covenant between God and Israel is familial at its core.

existence by way of natural means. God's plan for humanity to be fruit-ful and multiply has gone astray. Decay and corruption have broken into creation and the ultimate problem, then, is *death*. Abraham (and Isaac) exemplify this very problem. This is the issue that God is dealing with not only in Abraham's family, but also *through* Abraham's family.

God essentially adopts Abraham's family and makes it his own. Specif-ically, God makes a promise to Abraham that he will provide for Abraham a son. Abraham's first thought is that this problem can be solved through the human means of a surrogate. Abraham, however, is wrong. God will, by some miracle, provide a child for Abraham through Sarah. This, then, is a type of an *immaculate conception*. This is intended to prepare us for Jesus himself as the only begotten Son of God. We will get to this a bit later.

With this in front of us it becomes all the clearer that God is fulfilling his promise to renew the world through the framework of a *family*. God's plan is to address the cosmic problem and he does it through *covenant*. Once again, God is not creating a nation, but a family.

When we then progress from the familial covenant with Abraham to Sinai, the covenant takes on a political dimension. We see at Sinai that God is setting up not only a family, but also a nation of priests. The law of Moses (more on this in a moment) functions as a national constitution for Israel. Israel is a race, a political nation, but we must remember that God is also renewing his covenant that he initially made with Abraham, the father of this race that now stands before him at Sinai.

> This dimension is highlighted at the end of Exodus 2:23–25, which reads: During those many days the king of Egypt died, and the people of Israel groaned because of their slavery and cried out for help. Their cry for rescue from slavery came up to God. And God heard their groaning, *and God remembered his covenant with Abraham, with Isaac, and with Jacob.* God saw the people of Is-rael—and God knew (emphasis added).

This reality is confirmed in the language we find in Hosea 11:1–3:

> When Israel was a child, I loved him, and out of Egypt I called my *son*. The more they were called, the more they went away; they kept sacrificing to the Baals and burning offering to idols. Yet it was I who taught Ephraim to walk; I took them up by their arms, but they did not know that I healed them.

And in Exodus 4:22 we read, "Then you shall say to Pharaoh, 'Thus says the Lord, Israel is my firstborn son, and I say to you, "Let my son go that he may serve me." If you refuse to let him go, behold I will kill your firstborn son." We will see in subsequent chapters that this family metaphor carries right over to the king of Israel as not only the king, but also as the Son of God (see Ps 2:7).

This, then, is why Paul mixes metaphors for salvation in his own writing. Paul not only talks about Jesus as the king (Messiah), but as the one through whom believers received access to be members of the family of God. In Ephesians 2:19 Paul writes, "So then you are no longer strangers and aliens, but you are fellow citizens [kingdom metaphor] with the saints and members of the household of God [family metaphor]." We see this same kind of language in Romans. In Romans 4:11b–12 Paul says:

> The purpose was to make him [Abraham] the *father of all who believe* without being circumcised, so that righteousness would be counted them as well, and to make him *the father of the circumcised* who are not merely circumcised but who also walk in the footsteps of the faith *that our father Abraham* had before he was circumcised (emphasis added).

And most emphatically Paul writes in Romans 8:15–17:

> For you did not receive the spirit of slavery to fall back into fear, but you have received the Spirit *of adoption as sons*, by whom we cry, *"Abba! Father!"* The Spirit himself bears witness with our spirit that *we are children of God*, and if *children*, then heirs—heirs of God and fellow heirs with Christ, provided we suffer with him in order that we may also be glorified with him (emphasis added).

Paul isn't the only one to do this. John 1:12–13 says, "But to all who did receive him, who believed in his name, he gave the right to become children of God, who were born, not of blood nor of the will of the flesh nor of the will of man, but of God."

The bottom line is this: according to Paul (as well as other New Testament writers), salvation is the fulfillment of God's covenant with Abraham. God made a covenant with Abraham not as a political nation, but as a *family*. This means that we have the blending of both citizen and children language to conceptualize salvation when we encounter Sinai as the establishment of the first covenant and the cross as the establishment of the new covenant.

This perspective must shape the way we interpret what happened at Sinai when God established the covenant with Israel through Moses. *The predominant approach to interpreting Sinai is as the establishment of the judicial metaphor for salvation*. This is certainly true, but because of the concept of fictive kinship that links up with ancient Near Eastern covenants, we have to account for the fact that there is a *familial metaphor as well that plays a major role in the bigger picture of salvation*. In fact, the familial metaphor for salvation predates the judicial metaphor for salvation in the sense that God created covenants with Adam, Noah, and the patriarchs prior to the Sinai covenant. Not only this, but God delivered Israel from Egyptian slavery specifically because of his covenant with the patriarchs.

This foundation to Sinai is crucial for understanding Paul and his conceptualization of both salvation and holiness, because Paul's thinking about salvation, covenant, and kingdom largely hinges on his interpretation of how Jesus is the ultimate expression of God's covenant faithfulness.

Familial Metaphor, Covenant, and Holiness

So what impact does this have on holiness? We will develop this further, but let us say for now that if by entering into a covenant relationship with YAHWEH Israel is becoming members of the family of YAHWEH, then they must take on the very nature of their Father. The very essence of underlining the familial bond between Israel and YAHWEH *is holiness*. In being the sons of YAHWEH, Israel is to be the imprint of the nature of YAHWEH, just like with a father and son.

This is the ground on which the prophets build a case against Israel of violation of the covenant. Isaiah has this in mind when he preaches, "Ah, sinful nation, a people laden with iniquity, offspring of evil doers, children who deal corruptly! They have forsaken the LORD, the have despise the Holy One of Israel, the are utterly estranged" (Isa 1:4). Israel is supposed to be the window through which the world can witness the *otherness* of YAHWEH. Israel is to be nation of priests. Exodus 19:6a says, "and you shall be to me a kingdom of priests and holy nation." This is where Israel has failed and Jesus succeeds.

The Covenant Reveals God's Holy Nature and Humanity's Sin Nature

Without getting too far ahead of ourselves, however, we must explore *how the covenant is geared to reveal two things: (1) the holy character of YAHWEH, and (2) the sin nature*. This point becomes evident when we explore the function of the Mosaic law within the bigger picture of God's World Renewal Plan.

The Law and the Big Picture

So with the concept of fictive kinship at the core of the Sinai covenant, how does the law established at Sinai fit into the big picture for Paul, namely as it impacts *holiness as the ultimate expression of adoption*? This is the question we will wrestle with now.

Defining Torah

First, let us define what we mean by "law." "Law," in this context, finds its origins in the Hebrew word and tradition "Torah." The Hebrew word *tôrâ* ("Torah" henceforth) means "law" or "instruction."[14] It is also the title used in Jewish tradition to refer to first five books of the Old Testament. This is the most common usage of the term. When Jews talk about the Torah, they are usually referring to the first five books of Scripture (also known as the "Pentateuch").

At the same time, when Jews talk about "Torah observance" they are referring to observing the particular *laws and commands* laid out in the Torah which were given to Moses on the mountaintop at Sinai. This is the part of the Torah that is the "Mosaic law." This is a more specific usage of "Torah" as "law" as opposed to "Torah" as "Pentateuch." From here, we will use the phrases "Torah" and "Mosaic law" interchangeably. To refer to the first five books of the Bible, we will use "Pentateuch" rather than "Torah" to avoid confusion.

Torah as Mosaic law, then, is the formal law that is codified in the Ten Commandments and other laws that are the stipulations of the covenantal agreement between God and Israel. The question that we want to deal with now is how does the Torah reveal the sin-nature problem as well as the character of God?

---

14. See Koehler et al., *Hebrew and Aramaic Lexicon*, 1710. Also see "Torah" in Berlin and Brettler, *Jewish Study Bible*, 1–6.

The Torah Reveals

C. S. Lewis once wrote, "God whispers to us in our pleasures, speaks in our conscience, but shouts in our pain: it is His megaphone to rouse a deaf world."[15] Lewis expresses here that which is at the heart of the Torah: the means through which both the character of God and nature of man are revealed. The Torah responds to the reality that one of the great deceptions of sin is that it infects the moral compass. Sin makes the sinner believe that *there is nothing wrong.* The deadliest disease is that which hides just below the surface, going unnoticed so that will not be treated. If we're kept in the dark and confused about the fact that there may be something wrong, that disease will continue to work on us to numb us to the reality that we're dying.

The old adage goes, "Among the blind, the man with one eye is king!" The point here is that we judge our own state based on the people around us. This relates to the universal reality of death. Everyone dies. This is something that is simply a part of life. Without the good news, one would think that death was normal—that there was nothing wrong with it or unusual about it. This is bad practice. We are not to judge our own state by the people around us; rather, we are to judge ourselves on the holy, righteous, and pure character of the Creator.

Ultimately, what we're talking about is the same problem of Genesis 3: moral autonomy. In previous sections we saw that moral autonomy means determining for one's self what is good and what is evil. This is what Adam and Eve did in eating of the tree that God prohibited them to eat from. God said it wasn't good, they decided it was good, so they ate of it—moral autonomy.

So what does this have to do with the Mosaic law and the connection with the covenant theology? The giving of the Torah (*Shavuot*) is the moment in which God breaks into the dying world and sets in stone his standard for human living and posture of the heart. The Torah formally establishes the singular moral standard from Sinai. God lays out to an otherwise confused and sinful people what is good and what is evil.[16] Not only that, but he requires their adherence to that standard for the covenant relationship to continue. YAHWEH, through the exodus event and desert wanderings, is offering himself, as the Sovereign Creator of the *Cosmos*, as the patron deity of Israel, as the adopted Patriarch of Abraham's family.

15. Lewis, *Problem of Pain*, 91.

16. Herein lies the context for the doctrine of total depravity, which asserts that there is nothing good left in humanity. It also carries other implications about the blurring of the moral compass of humanity.

This links up to what Paul is talking about when he says:

> Now before faith came, we were held captive under the law, imprisoned until the coming faith would be revealed. So then, the law was our guardian until Christ came, in order that we might be justified by faith. But now that faith has come, we are no longer under a guardian, for in Christ Jesus you are all sons of God, through faith (Gal 3:23–26).

Paul is talking about the fact that when believers come to salvation through Christ, they are raised with Christ in the new reality of intimate indwelling of the Holy Spirit, who takes on the function that the Torah once had to convict of sin and guide the believer as well as the corporate people in holiness. This is the whole point of salvation: to establish a new humanity, a new creation, through a new covenant by the blood of the Messiah. In the new covenant, it is not the Word of God written on tablets of stone that outline for God's people what holy behavior looks like. No, it is the very Spirit of Jesus himself that indwells believers, thereby illuminating them to holiness of heart and life. This is why Paul is so adamant that God's people not "turn back again to the weak and worthless elementary principles of the world, whose slave you want to be once more? You observe days and months and seasons and years!" (Gal 5:9–10). Now that we have the Holy Spirit dwelling in us, we have a far superior way of knowing the will of God! We no longer need the external laws of the Torah to help us identify what's bad and what's good, or to help us understand that God is different, because we now have God himself dwelling in our hearts! To turn back to the law is to minimize the Holy Spirit!

Faith in Jesus that leads to the indwelling of the Holy Spirit arouses human senses. It also makes us sensible; it re-calibrates the moral compass. The Holy Spirit enables us to be able to identify our symptoms, our problems, and our sin. This is what Jesus meant when he said that the Holy Spirit would convict the world of its sin (John 16:8). The Holy Spirit isn't out to shame us, or embarrass us. No, the Holy Spirit's job is to bring us to our senses, to help us feel pain so that we can make the proper adjustments for healthy living. In pain, as Lewis reminds us, God speaks to us.

We also cannot fail to account for the fact that salvation requires repentance. Not a single one can be transferred from the kingdom of darkness to the kingdom of light without repentance. In turn, repentance requires conviction, and conviction, in turn, requires the *recognition that there is a problem with human behavior.*

So with this we see that the Torah (as well as the Holy Spirit) reveals God's expectations for human behavior. There is another dimension of revelation that goes beyond this that we cannot overlook and that is that God's prescription for human behavior reflects back on his own nature. That is, the kind of life that he expects from his people is to reflect the kind of God he is. If God required his people to commit adultery and abuse the poor, what kind of God would he be? If God required the oppression of women and the abuse of power, what kind of God would he be? If God required polygamy, what kind of God would he be?

On the other hand, if God required that his people selflessly love their neighbor as themselves, what kind of God would he be? If God required that his people take special care of the marginalized of society, like the orphan and widow, what kind of God would he be? If God required the sharing of resources for the good of the community at large over the good of the individual at the sacrifice of the community, what kind of God would he be? Finally, if God required that his people be a faithful, honest people, people with integrity who forgive seventy times seven times when wronged, what kind of God would he be?

The point I'm making is this: the Torah, in prescribing human behavior, not only reveals what God expects of his people, but also reveals what kind of God he is. He is a loving, just, merciful, gracious, and powerful God. He is the Good Creator. He is the Patron Deity of Israel.

Concerning the holiness of God, we would never know that there was a death-free and morally wholesome reality out there if our experiences were limited to the broken, decaying, and dying world of humanity. Once we see the holiness of God, we can understand that there is something different; there is a different reality. This principle is well at work in Isaiah 6:5 when Isaiah sees YAHWEH in his holiness that he shouts, "Woe is me! For I am a mean of unclean lips!" The law, by establishing God's standards for life, reveals that God is *different than this broken world*.

The Covenant As a Means for Sharing God's Nature

At this point there is a crucial connection to be made between behavior and nature. Living beings behave according to their nature. If God prescribes a certain kind of human behavior, it is for the purpose of reflecting a certain kind of nature. The people of Israel, by obeying the covenant commands of God (ethical code), are attesting to both their own nature as well as to the nature of God. This means that by adhering to the command to "be holy as God is holy," they are implying that God and his people *share the same character*. This, in turn, implies *sonship—family*.

The Torah as covenant stipulations given at Sinai, then, is intended to constitute a life of holiness for Israel. Along with this, the Torah is intended to reconstitute the image of God in Israel that was marred in Genesis 3. *It is at this very point that holiness as a vocation emerges* and the conversation links up with the NP. This is one of, if not *the*, central fresh perspective of holiness that we gain when accounting for the elements of interpretive priority given to us by the NP. We will explore this more in subsequent chapters.

The Hebrew text of the Old Testament attests to the fact that covenant code obedience is intended to testify to the holiness of God in Deuteronomy 6:4. Deuteronomy 6:4 is unquestionably the most cited text of the Old Testament among Jews. Deuteronomy 6:4 is known as the *Shema* (Heb. "hear") and encapsulates in a single statement the core theological value that makes Judaism unique among its ancient Near Eastern neighbors: *covenantal monotheism*. Israel was set apart from their neighbors because they were monotheistic creationists; they believed that there was one and only one true God who was the sovereign, morally absolute creator of the universe. This allowed for a singular ethic, a singular right to prescribe human behavior. Their obedience to the Ten Commandments was a testimony to the nature of that God.

Deuteronomy 6:4 reads, "Hear, O Israel, the Lord our God, the Lord is One." The Hebrew reads this way, *šěma' yisʾrāʾēl Yhwh ʾĕlôhênû Yhwh ʾeḥād*. What is striking is that in the ancient codices from which we translate the original Hebrew Old Testament, the last letter of the first word of the *Shema* and last consonant of the last word of the *Shema* are enlarged. Those letters are *ayin* and *dalet*. These two consonants, when read together, create the Hebrew word meaning "testimony."

This is an image of a *Shema* as it's found in the Masoretic Text. The top line comprises the enlarge consonants according to the centuries-old tradition.

So what does this tell us? Once again, it tells us that adherence to the Torah testifies to the nature of the One True God through *conformity to God's ethical standard as set forth in the law code*. When the prescribed behavior is performed, God's moral standard for humanity as the ordained authority over the creation becomes *visible to the world*. Israel, in other words, is the window for the world to witness the holy nature of the One True God. Israel is God's representative on earth. This was the same, original goal for all of humanity through the great gift of the image of God originating in the garden.. Israel is to be the image bearer in order to restore God's good order within the creation. We will see in just a moment, however, that Israel failed. This is key, as it will lead into Jesus playing the role of the True Israel in subsequent chapters. This, once again, is also where holiness as a vocation, as mission, is properly situated.

This truth of God's chosen people as the window through which the creation can see the true, holy character of God is an amazing and powerful. This same truth is valid for the church today. Jesus, as he ascends to his throne in heaven, leaves behind his disciples to represent him as the true king. They are to continue his work in inaugurating the kingdom of God on earth as it is in heaven. The church today is the testimony not only to the existence of God, but also to the *character of God*.

The issue that we run into, however, at the end of the Old Testament story is that the people of Israel have ultimately been unfaithful in properly observing the Torah. This is evidenced through several facts. First, the fifty or so years in Babylonian exile that occurs towards the end of the Old Testament attest to this. Second, even with the return to Jerusalem and the rebuilding of the temple that was destroyed in 587 BC, the glory of God returning among his people as depicted in Ezekiel still had not occurred. We read that the elders among those who returned to Jerusalem wept at the dedication of the rebuilt temple (Ezra 3:12–13). They wept because this new temple is a mere shadow of the temple and glory of God that was once with Israel.

When the Old Testament comes to a close, the people of God are still waiting. They are waiting for the Messiah; they are awaiting the fulfillment of God's promises to Abraham; they are awaiting God's glory to return among them; and finally, they are awaiting the new covenant promised by Jeremiah and Ezekiel.

We can summarize all of these by saying that Israel, at the close of the Old Testament, was still waiting for the inauguration of the kingdom of God through Israel. Even with their return to Jerusalem and the rebuilding of the temple of YAHWEH, they are a small and insignificant nation living at the mercy of the larger nations around them. They are waiting for God's promise to David to be fulfilled. They are waiting for the second exodus from their slavery because of their own sin. They are waiting for the kingdom of God to come.

This is why the Old Testament is a tragedy, because the Torah was ultimately unable to accomplish God's promises to Israel to bring about a nation of holy priests. The word of God that was written on tablets of stone, being external to human existence and not being able to penetrate the human condition in a living and dynamic way, was unable to restore the image of God in humanity as was intended since the beginning of the creation in Genesis.

This is precisely where the life of Jesus as the coming Messiah comes in during the first century. Jesus is the Living Torah and the true Israel who brings blessing to the nations through the family of Abraham, just as God promised. We will treat this subject thoroughly in the next chapter.

Conclusion

For Paul, the corporate people of God are the central point of reference for his thinking about salvation. God's World Renewal Plan is for a people, through a people. This interpretive posture is set against the tradition of interpreting Paul with the individual primarily in mind. We must remember, however, that Paul's *central purpose* in writing is *not* to answer questions about how individuals are saved. Rather, Paul's fundamental frame of reference for theology is the corporate people of God and God's World Renewal Plan through Jesus. Paul is primarily concerned with the *people of God* because this is always the emphasis of the Old Testament.

If corporate Israel as the covenant people of God is a central pillar of Pauline thought and theology, then all that Paul says should flow in and out of this concept. It is not only Paul's soteriology that hinges on the concept, but also his Christology and eschatology. In terms of Christology, Paul understands Christ primarily in terms of his mission as the fulfillment of God's mission to the people of God for the people of God. In terms of eschatology, Christ is the timely fulfillment of the promises to Abraham, Israel, and David, through whom the mission of God would reach the world.

A quick overview of some of Paul's priorities as evidenced by his letters shows us corporate Israel as the covenant people of God functioning in this central role for Paul's theology. In 1 Corinthians, the first problem Paul addresses with the church is unity. Paul accentuates not only the importance, but also the necessity of unity among new covenant members, because through Jesus they have been made a part of the corporate Christ in whom there are no divisions. In Galatians, Paul builds the case that circumcision (a symbol for obeying the letter of the law of Moses) is not the identifying mark of the people of God. Rather, it is faith in Jesus the Messiah that sets God's people apart as a holy people. *Paul is much less concerned with what makes one "saved" than he is with what makes one a member of the corporate body of Christ through the new covenant stipulations* (faith). In other words, to be saved is to be a member of the corporate Israel. They are one and the same.

The letter to the Romans has long been interpreted as systematic theology explaining how individuals are saved. Once again, these soteriological angles and dimensions are certainly present in Paul, but they are not the central thrust of Paul's message; they are secondary. Dynamics of individual salvation serve the master of ecclesiology for Paul. The thrust of Paul's message in Romans is to distinguish how the new covenant fulfills the old, how the new covenant impacts the eligibility of individuals to become members of the corporate people of God, and most centrally, how the gospel of Jesus Christ is the power by which what was once exclusive (excluding Gentiles) is made inclusive (including Gentiles). So once again, individual salvation is certainly a part of the dialogue, but the greater framework for the dialogue is the corporate people of God. Essentially, the NP contends that ecclesiology operates as the fundamental framework for Paul's thought and theology.

Unfortunately, this concept is far removed from the thought life of the average Christian interpreter of the Pauline corpus. We have inherited our interpretive posture from our Reformed tradition (including those of the holiness heritage). The dynamics of individual salvation have been the default point of reference for reading Paul. The average reader of Paul is looking for answers regarding how a person is saved or sanctified. Paul's letters, especially the letter to the Romans, undoubtedly answers such questions related to individual salvation; however, what Paul offers is a rather indirect response to that question.

So what does it mean that Paul's primary purpose in writing is almost always to address the "covenant people of God"? Paul's aim in writing is to bring his Gentile audience to understand their corporate identity in Christ. An critical element of Paul's soteriology is that "salvation" is the inheritance of the promises God made to Abraham. When we remove or neglect this element of Paul's thinking about salvation, we end up with an incomplete image of what salvation is, and specifically, how it is rooted in history and in God's work through a people. In other words, *for us today, salvation has become all too much about the individual and much less about the corporate body of Christ.* It's not all about Jesus and me! It is, however, all about God restoring his reign on earth through his chosen human agent.

With this interpretive framework in place we are able to get a fresh perspective of salvation. This is to say that the bulk of the Pauline corpus is intended to address questions for the people of God at large as identified by their relationship to Jesus as the Jewish Messiah. Unfortunately, most interpreters miss this point and end up focusing much more on the question of individual salvation as opposed to the concept of God saving a people, over and above the individual. Once again, we find this theme in Paul, but this theme is not the syllable on which the accent is intended to fall. We put the emphasis on the correct syllable by allowing this concept of God's covenant people to rest in the center of our interpretive lens. It is then that we're able to see much more clearly what Paul is telling the recipients of his letters.

The holiness heritage has continued the tendency to interpret Paul with the individual in mind. We almost always talk in terms of the holiness of the individual. This tradition comes to the holiness heritage *via* the interpretive framework of the Reformation. While it would certainly be irresponsible to neglect the dynamics of individual holiness, it would just as irresponsible to neglect Paul's equally important emphasis on holiness as it relates to the covenant people of God. If Paul's thinking about Christ's sanctifying work was much more focused on the corporate people of God than the individual, then it's time we put the emphasis on the right syllable. This is one of the primary issues needing to be addressed in bringing the holiness tradition into fresh perspective.

Part 2

Thy Kingdom Come

3

The Life of the King

The Living Torah and the True Israel

He regarded himself as having full authority to speak and act on behalf of God.

—E. P. SANDERS[1]

IN THE PREVIOUS CHAPTER we discussed how the concept of covenant is central to God's World Renewal Plan (which is synonymous with Paul's context for forming a soteriology). In that discussion we answered two questions. First, what is the Old Testament concept of covenant? And second, why is covenant theology important, especially for Paul? We said that covenant is the *means through which God executes his World Renewal Plan*. We also said that God's covenant faithfulness to Israel translates into God's redemption for Israel as well as redemption for rest of the *cosmos* in one fell swoop. We also noted that the covenant (i.e., Mosaic law or Torah) is a means through which God *reveals holiness as both the need for, and the goal of, the World Renewal Plan*. Finally, and most importantly, we said that when all of these dimensions of covenant telescope together it becomes clear that interpreting Paul *without* accounting for covenant theology results in a gross misinterpretation of the work of Christ as the Jewish Messiah. When we account for the covenant it becomes clear that the need and goal of redemption is *holiness*.

---

1. Sanders, *Historical Figure*, Kindle Location 4389 [ch. 15, paragraph 1].

In this chapter we will go a bit further by looking at how the *life of Jesus* fits into God's World Renewal Plan. We will answer the question, "Why did Jesus live?" The NP refreshes the memory of contemporary interpreters of the fact that Jesus is first and foremost the Jewish Messiah through whom God's World Renewal Plan is fulfilled. From this perspective we will find that the answer to our framing question (Why did Jesus live?) is that *Jesus' life ultimately reveals God's holy nature as well as his intended standard for human life.* In other words Jesus is the *Living Torah* and *the True Israel.*

How does this work? We said in the previous chapter that the Torah *reveals God's holiness as well as God's standards for human life.* We will see in this chapter that Jesus' life does the same. Jesus is the walking, living, breathing Torah who testifies to God's holy nature and his standards for the posture of the human heart. Prior to Jesus we could only see God through the witness of the Torah written on tablets of stone. Now, "in these last days he has spoken to us by his Son, whom he appointed the heir of all things, through whom also he created the world. He is the radiance of the glory of God and *the exact imprint of his nature,* and he upholds the universe by the word of his power" (Heb 1:2–3; emphasis added). The life of Jesus, then, has the same function as the Torah: to reveal "the radiance and the glory of God and the exact imprint of his nature."

What about Jesus as the True Israel? We will see in this chapter that where Israel failed in revealing the holiness of God *via* Torah obedience, Jesus is faithful. Jesus' faithfulness is the key God's very covenant fulfillment to Israel and his creation. The priority concept of Jesus as the Jewish messianic king goes hand in hand with Jesus as the Living Torah. In particular, *it is his chosenness, his "messiahship," which authorizes him as the imprint of the very nature of God.*

So what is the fresh perspective of salvation that we come away with in this chapter? We will see that the life of Jesus as the living model of the life of righteousness and self-giving love that he has come to share with his covenant people exemplifies the intended heart posture of the Christian. In other words, we will see that salvation is not just about what God does *in* his people, but also about he does *for* his people. Jesus is the example of what believers are to become as a result of God's covenant faithfulness to Israel through the cross.

The Gospel writers convey the life and teaching of Jesus as constantly pointing to the cross. This means that Jesus' identity and very character are inseparable from this redemptive act. It is in the cross that we witness the love of God in its clearest expression—self-sacrifice. Not simply self-sacrifice, but self-sacrifice as being a completely different way of engaging the world set against the human model of *incurvatus in se* (Latin, "being bent inward upon itself").[2]

At the same time, we must account for the fact that the cross simultaneously models the love of God *and the fulfillment of the mission of God.* These two are inseparable. This means that in looking at the life of Jesus as Living Torah as revealing the holy character of God and expectations for human life, we have to do so in light of Jesus' messiahship. In order to do this, we will look specifically at the notion of power as Jesus redefines it as the chosen king of Israel. We will see that the life of Jesus demonstrates what kind of kingdom he came to inaugurate—it is a kingdom of righteousness, holiness, justice, and peace. In order for this kingdom to come into power, the king submits his own life to death, even death on a cross. Jesus models human life as God intended it by redefining the concept of power. We will explore this further in this chapter.

Let us move forward, then, to explore the life of Jesus as presented in the Gospels in light of this first-century Jewish eschatological framework that brings these dimensions to front.

First-Century Judaic Eschatology

At the end of the previous chapter we noted that the story of Israel in the Old Testament is a tragedy. We said that it was a tragedy because of Israel's lack of faithfulness to YAHWEH manifest through failure to conform to the spirit of the Torah. We then listed the following expectations for Israel's deliverance in light of the tragedy: (1) God's glory to return to the temple, (2) deliverance from the ongoing exile, (3) the arrival of the Messiah, (4) the kingdom of God to come in its fullness.

These dynamics of Israel's expectations were alive and well within Second Temple Judaism. The Second Temple period was a pivotal time for Israel; it was also an awkward time for Israel. There were lots of questions needing answers. Second Temple and intertestamental literature evidences that there was a conviction among the Jews that they were indeed benefactors of the Abrahamic and Davidic promises, that they were characters on the stage of the great epic salvation narrative, and yet something was amiss. The Hebrew Bible ends with the book of Chronicles (in the Jewish

2. This Latin phrase was used by Martin Luther to describe the human fallen nature.

tradition) still looking forward to the great fulfillment of God's promises to Israel—the promise to be the means through which God's kingdom would be manifest on earth, the promise for a messiah, the promise for God's glorious presence to return to the temple, and the promise of a new covenant. God had once delivered his chosen people from slavery in Egypt and he could do it again. In fact, he would do it again because that is precisely what he promised.[3]

Linked to this hope for deliverance was the promise for a messiah to be born in the line of David. This Messiah, in the spirit of king David, would reestablish the rule and reign of Israel over the Gentile nations. Through David's seed, God's World Renewal Plan would be fulfilled. Through the Messiah, God would overthrow the reign of sin and death over the creation as well as that of unclean, Gentile nations over Israel.

This means that the Messiah was largely an eschatological political-religious leader. He was the great Jewish hope. He represented the dawning sun of the Day of the LORD, which meant God's people would inherit not only the Promised Land, but also the entire earth (cf. Ps 2 and 24:1). It also meant the restoration of the Davidic dynasty and the *cutting* of a new covenant promised in Jeremiah 31 and Ezekiel 36. All of these dimensions of God's World Renewal Plan link up in the great expectation for the Davidic king.

What we have described here is the landscape for the hope and expectations of Second Temple Judaism—the fulfillment of God's World Renewal Plan in the form of the reestablishment of the kingdom of God, through Israel, over the creation. All of this sets the context for understanding the message of the Gospels. This is the backdrop against which the Gospels unfold. This is the context for Jesus' arrival on the scene as the Davidic king who has come to put into place God's reign over the world.

There was something, however, that they missed. There was something about the ministry of the Messiah that they were not expecting. There was a beautiful and tragic twist in the narrative. We will get to that in the next chapter.

For now, let us turn to the Gospels with the proper background in place to see the life, ministry, death, and resurrection of Jesus as the culmination of God's World Renewal Plan—to see Jesus as the redeemer king.

---

3. This is the message of Isaiah 40. The message of Isaiah 40 was for an exiled people who awaited God's return. It is a call to celebrate the coming of Israel's God to deliver his people once again from their plight. The glory days of God's presence among his people filling the temple and reigning over the creation through Israel would come once again.

The Gospel according to the Gospels: God Is King

In restoring covenant as the primary point of reference for interpreting the Gospel accounts of the life of Jesus, the NP has also refocused the lens on the fact that Jesus is the messianic king. Of the various dimensions of Jesus' identity, it is his identity as the Messiah, the Davidic king, which is most heavily emphasized in the Gospels. If we were to ask, "What is the gospel according to the Gospels?" we would find that the thrust of the gospel is *the coming kingdom of God through the atoning work of the Messiah.* When we read the Gospels with the interpretive lens calibrated according to the NP specifications, we see this dimension of Jesus' life coming through the clearest and loudest.

This feature of the Gospels has been explored in its entirety numerous times and in numerous ways.[4] For this reason there is no need to detail it all out again here. There are, however, a few features of the Gospels that I wish to point out in highlighting the emphasis on Jesus as Israel's long awaited Davidic king. This will set the stage for looking at the life of Jesus as the act of redefining power and kingship, thereby modeling the holy nature of the kingdom.

Israel's King: Genealogy and Paul's Announcement of the Reigning King

In the very first pages of the collection of literature that we call the "New Testament," we have the attestation of Jesus' Davidic kingship. It is no accident that the New Testament begins with the genealogy of Jesus. Further still, it is no accident that the first verse of the New Testament reads, "The book of the genealogy of Jesus Christ, the son of David, the son of Abraham." Right out of the gate Matthew is telling his audience that this is the story of the central figure who is the fulfillment of God's World Renewal Plan through Israel—this is the *Messiah.* This is the one through whom God's covenant faithfulness to Israel will manifest. Matthew is telling us that Abraham's and David's story is also Jesus' story.

Matthew begins Jesus' genealogy with Abraham, unlike Luke who begins with Adam. This is Matthew's way of attesting to the Jewishness of

---

4. See Adams, *Parallel Lives*; Bock, *Mission Gospels*; Dunn, *Jesus Remembered*; Koester, *From Jesus to the Gospels*; McKnight, *King Jesus Gospel*; Stuhlmacher, *Gospel and the Gospels*; and Wright, *How God Became King*.

Jesus. Matthew, like Paul, is adamant that his audience understand that Jesus is the fulfillment of God's promises *first to Israel* (Rom 1:16). God didn't abandon his covenant promises to Israel! This story of Jesus is the *continuation of the story of Israel*. It was God's plan all along to renew the world and inaugurate his kingdom *through the family of Abraham*.

The genealogy comes to a climax in Matthew 1:17 which reads, "So all the generations from Abraham to David were fourteen generations, and from David to the deportation to Babylon fourteen generations, and from the deportation of Babylon to the Christ, fourteen generations." With this, Matthew is making it as clear as he possibly can. He is announcing that Jesus is the Davidic king, the Messiah who inaugurated the Day of the LORD and reestablished the reign of God on the earth. Three sets of fourteen is an especially Jewish combination of numbers. This tells us that this is not only *a* Jewish king; this is telling us that this is *the* Jewish king.

Along with this we cannot miss the most obvious of Matthew's claims that Jesus is the Messiah. Matthew calls Jesus the "Christ." When Jesus went by so many other titles (see below), it is "Christ" that is the most common designation for Jesus (more on the title "Christ" below). The central point of reference for introducing Jesus as the Messiah is *his kingship*.

Along with this we have the ambassador language of the New Testament to describe Jesus, which certainly attests to the kingship of Jesus. On the matter, Craig Evans writes:

> But of course, Paul is no ambassador in the eyes of the Roman Empire, any more than Jesus is a king. Nevertheless, Paul believes he is an ambassador in the truest sense, for he serves the true king and the true Son of God. Accordingly, he uses the language associated with the tasks of the ambassador: he must speak, declare, appeal, and intercede, to do and say whatever it takes, to make known the gospel, the good news of his king.[5]

Of all of the various dimensions of Jesus' identity it is apparent that Jesus is understood first and foremost as the Christ—the messianic king (Matt 16:16), the Lord of the *cosmos*. This is the title used for Jesus more than any other by New Testament writers. This is why even today we talk about "knowing Christ," and not "knowing the Prophet," or "knowing the Priest." We're following the model of Scripture when we do this. While priest and prophet certainly are indispensable messianic offices, the *central* messianic office is kingship. This messianic dimension of Jesus' identity has

5. Evans, "King Jesus," 133.

fixed itself in the life of the church because of the New Testament writers and their constant use of the title "Christ."

It is interesting, then, isn't it, that when we talk or think about the redeeming work of Christ, our minds do not typically go to kingdom first. We usually talk about substitutionary atonement. *This is priestly language.* This is sacrificial system language. This is Aaron language, not David language. At the same time, the designation of "Christ" calls on the messianic, *governing lordship* of Jesus. I don't say this to diminish the atoning work of Jesus, rather, to simply adjust the balance. Yes, Jesus is the Lamb of God that takes away the sin of the world. But, he is also the king who rules and reigns through his covenant people in righteousness and holiness.

Consider Romans 1:1–4:

> Paul, a servant of *Christ* Jesus, called to be an apostle, set apart for the gospel of God, which he promised beforehand through his prophets in the holy Scriptures, concerning his Son, who was *descended from David, according to the flesh and was declared to be the Son of God in power according to the Spirit of holiness by his resurrection from the dead,* Jesus *Christ* our Lord . . . (emphasis added)

This is Paul's greeting to the churches in Rome. Paul does something in this greeting that he doesn't do in his other letters. In this greeting, Paul defines the gospel. In doing so, Paul naturally talks about Jesus. Of all the ways that Paul could describe Jesus, his description of Jesus centers on two features of his identity: (1) the seed of David, and (2) the Son of God. This is a bit unusual. There are a number of ways that Paul could have described Jesus. Paul could have talked about the one who died on the cross, the one who gave his life for many, the one who was from Nazareth, the one who was born of a virgin Mary, etc. Why does Paul opt to point to Jesus being the son of David and the Son of God?

Normally, in our modern context, which is characterized by christological heresies that diminish the divinity or humanity of Jesus, we would read into this text that Paul is defending orthodox Christology. This may be what Paul is doing, but it's not likely. It is much more likely that Paul is pointing to the *kingship of Jesus.* Paul is underlining the fact that Jesus is the one through whom God became king. Notice that he calls Jesus "Christ" twice and even "Lord." This is governance language; this is Genesis 1–2 language.

We know that the church in Rome was made up of both Jews and Gentiles. We also know from the content of the letter that Paul was writing to the church in Rome in order to resolve the theological disputes amongst the two groups regarding covenant-people qualifications criteria. Paul points out right away that Jesus "was descended from David according to the flesh" (Rom 1:3) and is thereby accentuating the fact that Jesus is the long awaited messianic king, which in turn demonstrates God's faithfulness to Israel in fulfilling his promise that through them the world would have access to salvation.[6] God has been faithful to Israel and his faithfulness to Israel has resulted in the redemption of the world.

This isn't the only piece of information that Paul gives us. Paul also says of Jesus that he "was declared to be the Son of God in power according to the Spirit of holiness by his resurrection from the dead . . ." (Rom 1:4). Why is this important? If the first piece of information regarding God's faithfulness to Israel is more for the Jews, then this statement is more for the Gentiles (although both statements are certainly intended for both the Jewish and Gentile audience). Keeping in mind that Paul is writing to the church in Rome, we recognize that this is Caesar's city. This is the place from which Caesar rules the known civilized world. Not only this, but Caesar's claims about himself were quite lofty—he claimed to be the Son of God. This, according to Caesar, is what gave him the right to rule the world and advance his kingdom to the utter most extremities of the earth.

What becomes clear, then, is that for Paul, *Caesar personified the rule and reign of death over the creation.* In more eschatological terms, Caesar was the king of the *old evil age.* In that age, human rulers of the broken world reign through physical might, violence, aggression, oppression, and world colonization. Paul, in pointing out that *Jesus is the Son of God*, is doing much more than making a claim about the divinity of Jesus. *Paul is saying that it is Jesus, not Caesar, who reigns.* Jesus is the rightful Son of God. The proof is in the pudding: Jesus rose from the grave. Jesus' resurrection attests to the fact that he reigns over death. Paul fleshes this out later on in the letter to the Romans.

In this short greeting to the churches in Rome we find Paul underlining Jesus as king. He is the Davidic king who personifies God's faithfulness to Israel as well as to the entire *cosmos.* This reality also attests to the fact that Jesus has usurped the reign of sin and death by making a parody out of the Roman cross. Jesus, not Caesar, is the king. God has taken back what

6. See Isa 2:1–5 and Mic 4:1–3.

was rightfully his since the beginning. God's World Renewal Plan has come to a climax with Jesus.

But how does the life of the Messiah become the Living Torah? How is Jesus the True Israel? What does messiahship have to do with witness to the holy character of God? It is to these questions that we now turn.

The Messiah, Anointing, and Authorization for Ministry

The life of the Messiah as the ultimate testimony to the character of God is tied up in the etymology of the Hebrew word *mašîaḥ* The Biblical Hebrew concept of "messiah" has several dimensions. In a general sense, the noun "messiah" is a derivative of the Hebrew verb *mašîaḥ* which means, "to anoint with oil."[7] But what does it mean when someone is anointed with oil in a political-religious sense in the Hebrew Bible?

It means to be chosen.

An "anointed one" is *one who is chosen by God to accomplish a particular God-given task*. In other words, someone who has the anointing of God is "sanctified," or set apart. To accomplish the God-given task, the individual requires special empowerment by means of the Holy Spirit. The oil that is poured out on the chosen one symbolizes God pouring out his Holy Spirit (Heb. *rûaḥ*) on the individual for special empowerment.

It is precisely at this point that we are able to make the clear connection between *holiness and the mission of God*. To be sanctified is not only to be set apart with a heart that is fully circumcised, it is to be blessed with the powerful presence of the Holy Spirit to *accomplish a particular task or purpose*.

Historically it was prophets, priests, and kings who were anointed. Naturally, these roles required public authorization of their call to ministry. Authorization, as Moses models for us in the exodus narrative, comes through some sort of supernatural power. Again, this testifies to the fact that this individual has an especially vocational relationship with God.[8] An individual with that ability would have the anointing of the Holy Spirit that God alone can give. This is how authorization for ministry and *messiah* are linked.

---

7. Koehler et al., *Hebrew and Aramaic Lexicon*, 643.

8. This reminds me of the Roman centurion who, after experiencing the earthquake that followed Jesus' death on the cross, said, "Truly this was the son of God!" Creation is a witness to Jesus' identity.

By the time of Jesus, the term "messiah" had taken on a much narrower meaning. The term "messiah" became synonymous with "a future figure who will play an authoritative role in the end time, usually the eschatological king."[9] Leading up to the time of Jesus, the practice of anointing, or "messiah-ing" people, was most heavily connected with the royal court. Kings were anointed as specially empowered political leaders. This is crucial in understanding how Israel thought about themselves, their government, their king, and especially the king's unique relationship with YAHWEH as the patron deity of Israel. Along with this, the king of Israel, who was to reign over God's kingdom as his human agent, required the special empowerment and divine wisdom to rule in such a way that honored the very character of God. We get a clearer picture of this when we consider the Old Testament narratives involving anointing royal figures.

Jesus Redefines Power

Admittedly, the story of the original establishment of Israel's monarchy is a bit of a confusing read (1 Sam 8). Scholars have yet come to a consensus about what to make of it. The confusion comes from the fact that on the one hand it seems as if the establishment of the monarchy is a good thing, and on the other hand there is a strong sense of rebellion against the establishment of the monarchy and even God, at times, seems rather displeased about it. Running the risk of oversimplifying things, let me offer an interpretive solution.

I would suggest that the Scriptures are telling us that there is nothing wrong about the establishment of a monarchy in Israel. This is clear in the Torah where instructions are given for the future establishment of a monarchy (Deut 14–20). God never prohibits the establishment of a monarchy. To the contrary, he gives instruction as to how Israel's monarchy *should be different from the monarchies of the world*. It is good in that monarchy is a type of government that is an accurate reflection of the type of reign that God exercises over the creation. At the same time, the establishment of the monarchy is dangerous. It is dangerous because governing power is placed on the shoulders of a single person. Knowing the fallen state of humanity, there is great risk for the abuse of power. This means that whoever ends up as the king of God's people must have special wisdom for handling power

9. Collins, *Scepter and the Star*, 11.

in such a way that reflects God's very nature. *The king is to govern and lead the people in the same way that God himself governs and leads.*

Before getting ahead of ourselves, however, we must note that when Israel asks for a king (1 Sam 8), the reason that Israel gives for wanting a monarch is misguided. Israel asks for a human king because they want to be *like the nations around them* (1 Sam 8:7). This is a problem. This is problematic because since the exodus, God has been instructing his covenant people through Moses that their identity was to be found in being *different* from the Gentile nations. It is precisely non-assimilation that makes God's people unique. It was God's intention since the giving of the Torah that Israel be set apart, that they be different from other nations. For Israel to request a monarchy so that they could resemble the other nations simply evidences their hard-headedness. They still don't get it. They still don't understand that to be God's people is to be set apart from the world.

While God and Samuel both were frustrated with Israel's request, God instructs Samuel to grant their request. Thankfully, God is able to use evil intentions for the greater good (Gen 50:19–20). God's plan, as is revealed in the coronation of Jesus as king, is to take Israel's request for a king and *redeem it.* Thankfully, God is still able to set up his kingdom through human monarchy and all the while display his holiness to the world in terms that the world understands.

As the story progresses in 1 Samuel, we read about the coronation of Saul as the first king of Israel. Saul is the perfect king according to the world's standards. He comes from money (as demonstrated in the long genealogy) and the geographical location of his tribe (Benjamin) is perfectly centered between northern and southern Palestine. Most importantly, he is handsome and strong. Again, we have the concept of human power and influence perfectly personified in Saul. Saul, according to all accounts, is a man of power.

It doesn't take long, however, to see that Saul is, in fact, incompetent to lead God's people. Saul's faith is in his own humanness rather than in the Holy One of Israel. Saul uses secular means to lead God's holy priesthood. After all, it was by secular standards that he was chosen. The story that best illustrates the problem with Saul is the story of the battle with the Amalekites (1 Sam 15). This is the story where Saul was to wait for Samuel to perform the priestly ritual before taking the men into battle. As they wait for Samuel to arrive, fear overcomes the soldiers and many begin to abandon camp. The loss of soldiers leads Saul to think that he will be unable to win the battle. This is his first mistake. It is not by human might that battles are won. This is a human misconception. To the contrary, it is by the power of YAHWEH, the Creator God of Israel, that battles are won. Before long, Saul decides to perform that ritual himself so that they can enter into battle before losing more men. As Saul prepares the sacrifice, Samuel arrives and condemns him for disobedience.

So, what's the point? Again, Saul's faith is in human things. Saul is misled into believing that Israel is just like other nations—that power is in human might. From the outset, YAHWEH has been telling his people that their strength rests in their obedience to YAHWEH, the king of the *cosmos*. This is precisely the point of YAHWEH's word to Moses in facing the Red Sea in the midst of panic when he says, "The LORD will fight for you, and you have only to be silent" (Exod 14:14).

Saul's failure results in YAHWEH "tearing the kingdom of Israel" from him (1 Sam 15:28). There is a need for another king. This is where king David comes in. David is exactly the opposite of what human power looks like. Rather than being the firstborn, the one of privilege according to the world, he is the *last-born*. Not only is he the last-born, is the *eighth* son. Not only is he the eighth son, but he is also the one of the least privileged, consigned to watching over his father's sheep. He is so much the opposite of human power and influence that when Samuel asks to see Jesse's sons, he doesn't even call David. *David is an afterthought.*

Who does this sound like? Born in a manger? What good could come from Nazareth? What greatness is there in the son of a carpenter? *All of this demonstrates to the reader that God understands power and influence very differently than humans do.*

This is the point of the famous story of David and Goliath (1 Sam 17). David, who personifies weakness, inferiority, and insignificance (he's not even allowed to be a soldier!), stands off fearlessly against the giant sporting the world class man-made armor. Remember when David goes to put on Saul's armor and it doesn't fit? The storyteller is underlining that *David is not like Saul.* David doesn't fit into Saul's shoes. David is *different.* David believes that YAHWEH is his salvation, not human might or man-made armor. As David stands off against Goliath, he stands on his faith in YAHWEH as the deliverer and king of Israel who vindicates his people—David wins. David, then, becomes the *personification of the Messiah.* Because of David's faith that sets him apart as the one who *truly represents the power of Yahweh and the way in which Yahweh's power is manifest through humanity on earth, he becomes the anointed king of Israel.*

As David continues in his role as Saul's successor, we see that his faith is proven over time. David continues in his faithfulness to YAHWEH. As David finally becomes king (after much difficulty), his ultimate goal is to bring the Ark of the Covenant (which symbolizes the glorious presence of God) back to Jerusalem. As David's faithfulness is proven, God promises David that the Messiah will be born in his family, according to David's heritage of faithfulness.

With this, we have God's promise to David that his seed will be the one with the *eternal* anointing to rule over God's people. In this promise rests the concept of the messianic king—the Chosen One who will come from the family of David and faithfully rule by the Holy Spirit's empowerment with justice, righteousness, wisdom, and most importantly holy love. Isaiah, more than any other prophet, tells us about the Messiah and his reign. Isaiah quotes the Messiah with this:

> The Spirit of the Lord GOD is upon me,
>
> because the LORD has anointed me
>
> to bring good news to the poor;
>
> he has sent me to bind up the brokenhearted,
>
> to proclaim liberty to the captives,
>
> and the opening of the prison to those who are bound (Isa 61:1).

In this passage we have specific reference to the anointing of the Messiah by YAHWEH. Here we have Isaiah prophesying that the Messiah will be *marked by the empowerment of the Holy Spirit.* Following these first two lines we have the goal of empowerment: "to bring good news to the poor . . . bind up the brokenhearted, to proclaim liberty to the captives, and the opening of the prison to those who are bound." This tells us that the Messiah will be specially empowered as the chosen one of God for a ministry of deliverance and redemption. Once again, anointing and sanctification serve the purpose of *mission fulfillment.*

This is essential as this is where the NP on holiness comes into focus. The role and function of the Holy Spirit in this context is to *change the nature of a person,* thereby *endowing a person with a specific capacity to perform a specific task.* This is a bit different than how we traditionally think of holiness. Normally, when talking about holiness and the presence of the Holy Spirit, we make the connection with the *sanctifying work of the Holy*

Spirit. Once again, I'm not arguing that this *is not* correct; rather, that it is simply incomplete and missing the crucial dimension of *vocation*. *Holiness is not only about sanctification, it's about calling, vocation, and mission.*

We see this even in the baptism of Jesus. Upon his baptism by John, the crowd witnesses the dove that comes down to rest upon Jesus and anoint him for *ministry* (Matt 3:16). There is an even more evident example from the life of Jesus, one that is so obvious that we can't miss it. In other religions, often times "holy men" are considered those who sit and pray, meditate, and fast in isolation. This is intended to cultivate intimacy with God. Granted, Jesus certainly did this, however, this was the exception not the rule of Jesus' life. Jesus' life was spent *fulfilling his mission*. Jesus spent so much time fulfilling his messianic vocation that one of the major accusations of his enemies was violating the law of the Sabbath (Mark 3:1–16). What I'm saying is that Jesus, who is the perfect example of holiness, demonstrates the *holy life by fulfilling his mission*. Holiness and mission are inseparable.

In Isaiah, we not only find messianic prophecies that deal with the delivering work of the Messiah, but also descriptions of which kind of ruler the Messiah will be. In Isaiah 9:6–7 we read:

> . . . and the government shall be upon his shoulder,
> and his name shall be called
> Wonderful Counselor, Mighty God,
> Everlasting Father, Prince of Peace.
> Of the increase of his government and of peace there will be no end,
> on the throne of David and over his kingdom,
> to establish it and to uphold it
> with justice and with righteousness
> from this time forth and forevermore.
> The zeal of the LORD of hosts will do this.

> In a very similar vein we read this from Isaiah 11:1–4a:
> There shall come forth a shoot from the stump of Jesse,
> and a branch from his roots shall bear fruit.
> And the Spirit of the LORD shall rest upon him,
> the Spirit of wisdom and understanding,
> the Spirit of counsel and might,
> the Spirit of knowledge and the fear of the LORD.

And his delight shall be the fear of the LORD.

He shall not judge by what his eyes see,

or decide disputes by what his ears hear,

but with righteousness he shall judge the poor,

and decide with equity for the meek of the earth.

In this passage Isaiah brings together the two dynamics of Holy Spirit: empowerment and wise governance. The Messiah is both a deliverer *and* a king. He is anointed; he is chosen for the task of deliverance from the enemies of the people of God as well as to rule over his delivered, covenant-kingdom people. He will not rule like secular world government;; he will rule according to God's wisdom and righteousness.

The powers of the world, in the Gospels and during the first century for Jews, were personified by Rome. Rome, like all earthly kingdoms, advanced her power, influence, and wealth by violence and might. *The kingdom of God is different as is God's king.* This is evident through Isaiah's description of the nature of the Messiah's reign over the earth. For Isaiah, there is a deep connection between royalty and servanthood. In describing this theme in Isaiah, John Oswalt writes, "God's solution to the cruelty and oppression of the world is not to be more cruel and oppressive, but, as 52:13—53:12, the last of the so-called Servant Songs, shows, it is to take that cruelty and oppression into himself and give back love. This is ultimate power."[10]

This concept of power through weakness and servanthood is essential for understanding the establishment of God's reign through the cross. E. P. Sanders writes,

> In the end the early Christians kept the title "Messiah" but rede-fined it to accord with their own experience: Jesus became for them a new kind of messiah, one who had acted as a miracle-worker and prophet during his lifetime, but who was also the heavenly Lord who would return at the end. This definition of messiah — prophet, miracle-worker and heavenly Lord — is *post factum*: the early Christians viewed him in this way and also called him "mes-siah." As far as we know, the term "messiah" had not been defined in such a way in advance.[11]

---

10. Oswalt, *Isaiah*, 45.

11. Sanders, *Historical Figure*, Kindle Location 4481–4485 [chapter 15, section 1, paragraph 11].

The passage indicates that the humility and obedience of the servant is key to efficacious redemption. Functioning within the context of the book at large, the servant of YAHWEH (at least in this Servant Song) epitomizes the nature of human influence and power as intended by the transcendent Creator. Going against the broken human understanding of power, the prophet teaches that human value is inseparable from a submissive and intimate relationship with YAHWEH. YAHWEH is the one who is able to work powerfully in history. Humanity has a choice to participate humbly in YAHWEH's work. Furthermore, YAHWEH's competency is such that he is able to even use the injustices and corrupt behavior of fallen humanity to redeem the world. His redemption, however, comes to humanity through his faithful and obedient one who is faithful to the point of death, even death on a Roman cross. Those who fully entrust themselves to YAHWEH will be exalted and they will be exalted by the Holy One of Israel because of their faith and obedience. With a great deal of clarity, we will see these same dynamics at work in the Philippians passage.

More specifically, God's vision of power and influence is diametrically opposed to the world's idea of power and influence. The criteria for exaltation eligibility in the kingdom of God is set in contrast to the criteria of the world. Human power was characterized by military might, coercion, and dominance in a time of Assyrian aggression, the rise of the Babylonian empire, vassal rebellions and political alliances. Throughout the entirety of Isaiah's ministry, he speaks out against such a view of human leadership because of its great disharmony with the nature of the Holy One of Israel. The Suffering Servant depicts a leader whose influence is not earned through might, political manipulation or strategic alliances with pagan nations, but through *weakness and submission* to YAHWEH. It is the one whom the world would not even think to look upon that the Holy One of Israel uses powerfully for his purposes in the world. This goes on to connect with the greater section of 40–66 to communicate that God's transcendent plan for redemption further proves that he is uniquely God.

The servant of YAHWEH knows his Lord enough to trust that he is capable of redeeming any and all human behavior—even acts of injustice. In response to the loyalty of the servant, YAHWEH is able to fully redeem the detestable act of humanity, thus demonstrating exactly what YAHWEH is capable of accomplishing. This proceeds to communicate that the servant merits exaltation based on two things: (1) humble faithfulness and trust in

YAHWEH and (2) offering himself as the instrument for redemption of his enemies.

At this point you'll notice that the complete "submission to YAHWEH" language resonates with submitting to YAHWEH's moral autonomy. It's understood, then, that the servant of YAHWEH recapitulates the act of human moral autonomy that we find in Genesis 3 that caused death, decay and corruption to enter into the creation. Jesus, to the contrary, is completely submissive to the will of YAHWEH, even when YAHWEH leads him to death. He trusts and believes that what his Lord decrees as "good" is good indeed. Jesus' complete obedience, then, undoes what Adam and Eve did in allowing sin and death to enter the world. Jesus' complete obedience and submissiveness to YAHWEH is the life through which righteousness enters into this fallen world. This is the concept at the heart of Romans 5:17 which reads, "For if, because of one man's trespass, death reigned through that one man, much more will those who receive the abundance of grace and the free gift of righteousness reign in life through the one man Jesus Christ." Jesus undid Adam's folly.

There are two other places in the Old Testament that further demonstrate the nature of power in the kingdom of God. The first is a part of the story of the exodus. In the beginning of the book of Exodus, we find Pharaoh brutally oppressing God's people. As a result, Israel cries out for help to the God of their fathers. Because God is entirely faithful to his promises, he responds to their cry for help. What is his solution to bring deliverance from the oppression of the mighty pharaoh? Moses, a helpless baby. John Oswalt says this:

> God did not devise some vast political plan or military strategy to deliver his people from bondage. Instead, he chose to use a baby— a creature so helpless that he could not exist for long away from his mother's breast, a baby so vulnerable that his parents had to hide him in a basket, in a swamp.[12]

The second passage from the Old Testament is almost precisely the same as this one, but we find it again in the book of Isaiah.[13] The Gospel writers cite this verse as a prophecy foretelling the virgin birth of Jesus. The Gospels writers, being under the inspiration of the Holy Spirit, certainly

12. Oswalt, *Exodus*, 29.

13. You will notice that much of what the Old Testament says about holiness and servanthood and how these things fit into God's World Renewal Plan is found in the book of Isaiah.

got it right. There is another message, however, that is linked up with this verse that stands in the shadow of the Christian application of this verse to Jesus as the Messiah. This second interpretation we can discover only when we consider the greater literary and historical context in which Isaiah 7 unfolds.

The atmosphere in this passage in Isaiah 7 is deep fear. The issue at hand is that the kingdom of Judah is being threatened by its neighbors to the north who have formed a coalition (Syro-Ephraimite coalition) to defend themselves against the growing army of Assyria. This coalition wants Judah to join them in order to strengthen their chances against the much larger and stronger Assyria. If Judah doesn't join them, they will attack Judah, kill the king (Ahaz), and place a puppet king in his place. This is why King Ahaz is afraid. We know that Ahaz is afraid because the prophet Isaiah tells him directly, "Be careful, be quiet, do not fear, and do not let your heart be faint because of these two smoldering stumps of firebrands . . ." (7:4). It is not only Ahaz who is afraid, but all the people of Judah as well! The text says, "the heart of Ahaz and the heart of his people shook as the trees of the forest shake before the wind" (7:2b).

In the midst of warring, violence, human threat, manipulation, and fear, God speaks. He sends his prophet Isaiah to King Ahaz to give him a sign that will bring comfort, a sign that communicates the fact that Ahaz should put his fear to death. Now in a context like this, one would expect the sign to be something such as a legion of angels, or chariots and horses, a strong sword for battle, a firm shield for protection, some sort of sign that communicates that the all-powerful God of the universe is on his side. But no! What sign does he give him *but a newborn baby*! This is counter-intuitive to human thinking. Of all things that symbolize power, a baby is certainly not one of them.

So what's the point? The point is that God's power is perfect in weakness. God can do more with a helpless baby than any man can do with legions of soldiers riding into battle, fully clothed in armor on the greatest stallions. This is the idea behind the name *Emmanuel*. We all know that this name means "God with us" in Hebrew. However, it's deeper than this. God's presence with us is most effective in power with trust, with weakness and submission to his will.

The life of Jesus falls right in line with this. God's greatest, most powerful redemptive act in human history is manifest through the weak, submissive act of the Messiah. The Messiah demonstrates his greatest power through his own weakness and submission. This submission resulted in the fulfillment of God's World Renewal Plan, the fulfillment of the mission of God, and simultaneously the great witness to the holy love of God. This is salvation in fresh perspective.

This dynamic is heavily present in Jesus' words, "*Eli, Eli, lema sabachthani*" (Matt 27:46). This statement has been a bit of an enigma for interpreters for centuries. The challenge of interpretation, once again, comes with Old Testament illiteracy. Many New Testament readers miss the fact that Jesus is citing Psalm 22:1 when he says this.

When one reads all of Psalm 22, the parallels between the circumstances (poetically) described by the psalter (David) and Jesus on the cross are staggering. The major difference is that in Psalm 22, David uses figurative speech but for Jesus it is literal. See Table 1 for the comparisons.

Table 1

David in Psalm 22	Jesus in the Crucifixion Narrative
But I am a worm and not a man, scorned by mankind and despised by the people. All who see me mock me; they make mouths at me; they wag their heads; "He trusts in the LORD; let him deliver him; let him rescue him for he delights in him!" (22:6–8)	And they stripped him and put a scarlet robe on him, and twisting together a crown of thorns, they put it on his head and put a reed in his right hand. And kneeling before him, they mocked him, saying 'Hail, the King of the Jews!' And they spit on him and took the reed and struck him on the head. And when they had mocked him, they stripped him of the robe and put his own clothes on him and led him away to crucify him. (Matt 27:27–31) And those who passed by derided him, wagging their heads and saying, "You who would destroy the temple and rebuilt it in three say, save yourself! If you are the Son of God, come down from the cross." So also the chief priests, with the scribes and the elders, mocked him, saying "He saved others; he cannot save himself. He is the King of Israel; let him come down not from the cross, and we will believe in him. He trusts in God; let God deliver him now, if he desires him. (Matt 27:39–43)
I am poured out like water, and all my bones are out of join; my heart is like wax; it is melted within my breast; my strength is dried up like a potsherd, and my tongue sticks to my jaws; you lay me in the dust of death. (22:14–15)	After this, knowing that all was now finished, said (to fulfill the Scripture), "I thirst." (John 19:28).
For dogs encompass me; a company of evildoers encircles me; they have pierced my hands and feet. (22:16)	And they crucified him ... (Matt 27:35)
. . . they divide my garments among them, and for my clothing the cast lots. (22:18)	And when they had crucified him, they divided his garments among them by casting lots. (Matt 27:35)

The theme of Psalm 22 is trust. While at first glance this Psalms seems like a lament, but it isn't! The thrust of this psalm is the fact that *even though the psalmist suffers, he will trust in* YAHWEH. This is the heart of holiness and at the heart of saving faith. Jesus, by quoting Psalm 22, is declaring that even though his submission and obedience to YAHWEH has landed him in excruciating pain on the cross, *he still trusts in his Father.*

This runs parallel to Isaiah's song of the Suffering Servant (Isa 52:13—53:12). The Suffering Servant, by being obedient, weak, and submissive, ends up being the means through which God's redemptive work is manifest for the covenant people of God.

There is an even stronger statement of faith in Isaiah 50:4–9, which reads:

> The Lord GOD has given me the tongue of those who are taught, that I may know how to sustain with a word him who is weary. Morning by morning he awakens; he awakens my ear to hear as those who are taught. The Lord God has opened my ear, and I was not rebellious; I turned not backward. I gave my back to those who strike, and my cheeks to those who pull out the beard; I hid not my face from disgrace and spitting.

This also runs parallel to what Paul says in Philippians 2:5–8:

> Have this mind among yourselves, which is yours in Christ Jesus, who, though he was in the form of God, did not count equality with God a thing to be grasped, but emptied himself, by taking the form of a servant, being born in the likeness of men. And being found in human form, he humbled himself by becoming obedient to the point of death, even death on a cross.

Here, as in Isaiah 52:13—53:12, Paul highlights the perfect obedience of Jesus that goes hand in hand with submissiveness and the emptying of power. It is because of Christ's complete obedience and weakness that his redemptive work is efficacious. *This means that salvation and holiness as a heart-posture as well as a vocation go hand in hand; they are two sides of the same coin. Through weakness, submission, humility, and obedience, the power of God comes to life in the world through his human agents for the cause of his redemptive purposes.*

This heart-posture, this sort of behavior that is modeled by Jesus, is the cure to the human problem revealed in the Old Testament. The Old Testament, through the Torah, revealed that the problem with humanity is moral autonomy. Even our bones cry out, "I will do it my way!" We are a rebellious people with an ego that has run amuck. What is the solution? Submission, weakness, obedience, and ultimately love.

Jesus, the True Israel

Flowing directly from the complete obedience of the Messiah comes our final and most important point about the life of Jesus and that is the life of Jesus as the *True Israel*. We said in the previous chapter that the Torah was designed to reveal the character of God as well as the sinfulness of humanity. The Torah was successful in revealing the sinfulness of humanity; however, it failed in revealing the holy character of God *to the world* because of Israel's disobedience. Not only this, but also because of the tragedy of Israel, the kingdom of God had yet to come in its fullness. In this sense, the Torah was not able to complete what it set out to do. Jesus, as the Living Torah, puts on display for the entire world to see the holiness of God. It is through the life of Jesus that this is accomplished.

All of the features of power through obedience evidence this reality. Through the special empowerment of the Holy Spirit given to the Messiah, he is not only endowed with the ability to fulfill his vocation, but the anointing of the Holy Spirit authorizes him as the window into the divine character, the one who truly manifests the characteristics of the One True God, the God of Israel.

This reality comes through the sonship language used to describe the Messiah in the Old Testament. The Messiah is no ordinary king (which we already saw through the example of how "power" translates into the kingdom of God through the Messiah); he is the king of Israel whose patron deity is the God of the universe. Because of this, there is a connotation that the king, being the preeminent one of God's people, would carry out God's reign among his people. In doing so, the king had to reflect the nature and character of God, especially as it pertains to ruling and governance. What we are talking about here is the same thing that we talked about in previous chapters: the *vocational dimension of the image of God in humanity*. The image of God in humanity was intended to be the point of calibration for human behavior as the privileged ones who are to reign in the created world out of divine wisdom and love. In much the same way, the anointing of the Holy Spirit of God on the king is intended to manifest the *image of God in the king*. If the king is the Messiah, the chosen one, then the king can be conceptualized as the "Son of God"—the one who bears God's image.

Psalm 2:7 attests to this when we hear the Messiah say, "I will tell of the decree: the LORD said to me, You are my Son; today I have begotten you." The king of God's chosen people is the Son of God in the sense that he represents God's holy character through kingdom ruling on behalf of the patron deity.

This concept, however, takes on a literal dimension with Jesus. Jesus is the *actual begotten Son of God.* As Paul points out, Jesus' true identity as the Son of God is ultimately revealed through his resurrection. Paul says in Romans 1:3–4, "concerning his Son who was descended from David according to the flesh and was declared to be the Son of God in power according to the Spirit of holiness by his resurrection form the dead, Jesus Christ our Lord . . ."

This importance of the sonship of Jesus is multifaceted. Here in this context, however, we must take note of the *revelatory importance of the sonship of Jesus.* The fact that Jesus, as the Son of God, reveals the holy character of God cannot go overemphasized. This is what the writer of Hebrews is talking about when he says this:

> Long ago, at many times and in many ways, God spoke to our fathers by the prophets, but in these last days he has spoken to us by his Son, whom he appointed the heir of al things, through whom also he created the world. He is the radiance of the glory of God and the *exact imprint of his nature,* and he upholds the universe by the word of his power (Heb 1:1–3a; emphasis added).

It is by no coincidence that the writer here chose "Son" rather than another designation for Jesus in this context. The writer is emphasizing that it is *inherent to sonship to share the nature of the Father.*

Jesus, then, is the True Israel and the Living Torah. He is the one who rightly and accurately reveals God. There is the famous story of the conversation that occurs between Jesus and his disciples in John 14:7–11. It goes like this:

> "If you had known me, you would have known my father also. From now on you do know him and have seen him." Philip said to him, "Lord, show us the Father, and it is enough for us." Jesus said to him, "Have I been with you so long, and you still do not know me, Philip? Whoever has seen me has seen the Father. How can you say, 'Show us the Father'? Do you not believe that I am in the Father and the Father is in me? The words that I say to you I do not speak on my own authority, but the Father who dwells in me does

his works. Believe me that I am in the Father and the Father is in me, or else believe on account of the works themselves."

Once again, Jesus is teaching that he reveals God the Father. This is the nature of his sonship. This is the nature of his obedience, obedience to death, not only death, but death on a cross. It is to the cross now that we turn.

4

The Cross and the New Covenant

In the messianic events of Jesus' death and resurrection Paul believes *both* that the covenant promises were at last fulfilled *and* that this constituted a massive and dramatic irruption into the processes of world history unlike anything before or since. *And at the heart of both parts of this tension stands the cross of the Messiah, at once the long-awaited fulfillment and the slap in the face for all human pride.* Unless we hold on to both parts of this truth we are missing something absolutely central to Paul.

—N. T. WRIGHT[1]

IN THE PREVIOUS CHAPTER we looked at how the life of Jesus fits into the larger framework of God's World Renewal Plan. We said that Jesus' life is a testimony to the kind of kingdom that he came to inaugurate. We said that Jesus was the Living Torah of God that testified both to the nature of God as well as the ethical standards for the people of God. The kingdom of God, Jesus showed, was a holy kingdom, a kingdom of grace, mercy, forgiveness, self-giving love, and righteousness (we will flesh out the righteousness bit in the next chapter). As the Living Torah, Jesus brings to life the nature of God that was previously written on tablets of stone. Finally, we said that all of these dimensions of Jesus as the Living Torah meant that Jesus is the True Israel.

In this chapter, we will move forward by evaluating how the death of Jesus fits into God's World Renewal Plan. We will answer the question,

1. Wright, *Paul in Fresh Perspective*, 54; emphasis added.

"Why did Jesus die?" We will lend special attention to the death of Jesus as the pinnacle event of God's covenant faithfulness to Israel by solving the sin-death problem for both Israel and Gentiles (as well as the *cosmos* at large) by fulfilling the stipulations of the Torah. Finally, we will see that the willing death of the Son of God is the exemplary testimony to holiness as well as the great divine act of justice to Israel and to the world.

So what of our fresh perspective of salvation? We will see that the death of Christ, as the crucial event of forgiveness and reconciliation between the *cosmos* and its Creator, provides a means through which the indwelling of the Holy Spirit for the transformation of the human heart is made possible. In terms of the covenant, the blood of Christ shed on the cross is the fulfill-ment of the "cutting" of the new covenant in which believers, through faith, can become members of the family of God (fictive kinship); this means taking on the very nature of the Father and the image of God as a vocation restored. We will also begin to see the corporate dimensions of holiness and salvation through the mystery of God's plan to facilitate the incorporation of Gentile believers into Abraham's family of faith through saving faith in the Lordship of Jesus Christ.

Jesus as the Second Moses and the Cross as the Second Exodus: The Inauguration of a New Covenant

Many contemporary readers of the New Testament overlook the fact that God fulfills his promise to Israel for a new covenant through the cross. Normally, when we consider the cross, all we see is substitutionary atone-ment—Jesus died for our sins. And yes, of course, Jesus' redemptive death makes provision for the sin-guilt of believers; *but it also accomplishes much more than that.* The death of Jesus establishes an entirely new point of refer-ence for the covenant people of God. This concept is crucial for Paul, as the NP has reminded us. So often, when Paul talks about the "mystery" of the Gospel, he's referring not only to the mystery of the death of the Messiah, but also to the mystery of the fact that God's plan all along was to create a means through which Gentiles could (easily) be incorporated into the holy people of God.

This issue has holiness written all over it. We mentioned before that Jewish identity is wrapped up in non-assimilation. This reality finds its origins in the Old Testament; we find this in food laws, marriage laws, cir-cumcision, Sabbath observance, etc. So many of the Torah commandments function as *object lessons* to Israel, teaching them that they are to be set apart from Gentiles; Jews are clean, Gentiles are not. This concept erases the very principle that constitutes Jewish identity. If Judaism finds its identity in reciprocal determination through binary opposition with Gentiles, then to make Jews and Gentiles alike is to remove the counterpart that constitutes identity. If there is no "other," then we are no one if identity is dependent upon the existence of the other.

So, once again, this idea that Gentiles can partake in the heritage of Israel through faith in the Messiah is an indispensable dimension behind what Paul means by the "mystery" of the Gospel of Jesus Christ (Eph 3:1–13). N. T. Wright adds that,

> Paul developed something we can appropriately call his "theology," a radical mutation in the core beliefs of his Jewish world, because only so could he sustain what we can appropriately call the "worldview" that he held himself and that he longed for his churches to hold as well. Other worldviews have their sustaining and shaping practices, but for Paul these markers (circumcision, the food laws, and so on) had been set aside as inappropriate for the new messianic day, for the new messianic people. Only a robust reappropriation of the Jewish *beliefs*—monotheism, election and eschatology, all rethought around the Messiah and the spirit—would do.[2]

This is what Paul has in mind when he writes this in Ephesians 3:4–6:

> When you read this, you can perceive my insight into the mystery of Christ, which was not made known to the sons of men in other generations as it has now been revealed to his holy apostles and prophets by the Spirit. *The mystery is that the Gentiles are fellow heirs*, members of the same body, and partakers of the promise in Christ Jesus through the gospel (emphasis added).

We see this in 1 Corinthians 2:8–13 as well:

> None of the rulers of this age understood this, for if they had, they would not have crucified the Lord of glory. But, as it is written, "What no eye has seen, nor ear heard, nor the heart of man imagined, what God has prepared for those who love him—," these things God has revealed to us through the Spirit For the Spirit searches everything, even the depths of God. For who knows a person's thoughts except the spirit of that person, which is in him?

2. Wright, *Paul and the Faithfulness of God*, 1:xvi.

So also, no one comprehends the thoughts of God except the Spirit of God. Now we have received not the spirit of the world, but the Spirit who is from God, that we might understand the things freely given us by God. And we impart this in words not taught by human wisdom but taught by the Spirit, interpreting spiritual truths to those who are spiritual.

Paul notes that this concept is such a mystery that the Holy Spirit alone can do an adequate job of communicating it to the human heart. This makes for a certain degree of intrigue when dealing Peter's story in Acts. When Peter was first baptized by the Holy Spirit at the beginning of the book of Acts, he has clearly become a new person and has gained spiritual insight as to the purpose of the death of Jesus—something that he didn't understand before. All of the sudden, with the help of the Holy Spirit, it clicks for Peter. Peter suddenly understands why Jesus had to die and raise again as the Messiah. It seems almost as if Peter has it all figured out in the moment that the Holy Spirit rushes upon him. This isn't the case, however.

Do you remember the story of Cornelius in Acts 10? Peter is praying on the roof at Simon the Tanner's home when he has a vision. In that vision, Peter sees a series of unclean animals and God instructs Peter: "Rise, Peter; kill and eat" (Acts 10:13). Peter, shocked at such a command, says, "By no means, Lord; for I have never eaten anything that is unclean." The text continues, "And the voice came to him again a second time, 'What God has made clean, do not call common'" (Acts 10:15). Peter doesn't really know what to make of this until he gets a message to go to a Gentile's home. To make a long story short, Peter then goes to witness Cornelius, a Gentile believer, receive baptism of the Holy Spirit. At this point Peter declares, "Can anyone withhold water for baptizing these people, who have received the Holy Spirit just as we have?" (Acts 10:34b).

This story demonstrates that Peter's theology still needed some adjustment even after being baptized by the Holy Spirit. The thought never occurred to him, even in his enlightened mind, that Gentiles could become members of the covenant people of God *simply through* faith in Jesus the Messiah. This is the mystery that Paul is talking about over and over again.

This is the mystery of the new covenant. Not only does the new covenant purify the heart and launch the kingdom of God, but it also creates a means for Gentiles to partake in the heritage of Israel.

The Cross as the Second Exodus

So how does the cross set up and constitute a new covenant? Furthermore, where in the Scriptures do we find proof of this? All throughout the gospels the cross is presented as the second exodus and Jesus as the second Moses. This is crucial for tying together the various threads of the greater tapestry that is God's World Renewal Plan. It is through the cross that the new covenant, promised by the prophets Jeremiah and Ezekiel, is established. It is also through this new covenant that the kingdom of God is launched on earth as it was originally intended through the first covenant with Israel made at Sinai through the giving of the Torah.

Jesus, like David, is monarch of God's chosen people. At the same time, Jesus, like Moses, is the leader of a great rebellion against the pagan nations of the world (for the exodus, this is personified in Egypt and Pharaoh, for the cross, Rome and Caesar). Moreover, Jesus, like Moses, is a covenant-maker. This means that in Jesus we have the telescoping of two historical-political leaders: David and Moses.

But how do these two fit together? As noted in the previous chapter in the section on first-century Judaic eschatology, many first-century Jews believed Jesus to be the long-awaited messianic king. The expectation was for the Messiah to establish a Jewish empire that would reign and rule the nations of the earth. More to the point, the messianic empire was expected to exercise dominion over the pagan nations of the world. The pagan nations would submit to the hegemony of Israel and the God of Jacob. As a precursor to all of this, the Jewish Messiah was expected to lead a rebellion against the pagan rulers of the world that reigned over and oppressed God's covenant people. The kingdom was to come as a result of Israel's rebellion against her oppressors; first deliverance, then kingdom—first war, then peace. Wright, once again, sums it up well with this,

> Many Jews of Paul's day were in fact thinking in terms of a "new exodus," a great new act of God through which Israel would be freed from oppression. Paul agrees with this expectation, but instead of seeing it in terms simply of political freedom from Rome, he translates it into the ultimate freedom: the liberation of the whole cosmos from sin, corruption and death.[3]

How this all works becomes much clearer when we remember the story of the exodus. The exodus is the critical, nation-defining moment for

---

3. Wright, *Paul for Everyone*, 99.

Israel. The Israelites were Pharaoh's slaves when God sent Moses to deliver them from Pharaoh's brutal oppression (described in Exod 1–2). Moses, the one sent by God, performed miracles in public to demonstrate that he was the chosen one of God who had been given God's authority to accomplished the task of delivering Israel from her oppressor.[4] Then, through Moses, God initiated the rebellion by sending an onslaught of destructive plagues against Pharaoh and Egypt. The plagues eventually forced Pharaoh into a position where he had no choice. He let Israel go.

After successfully leading the rebellion against Pharaoh (and thereby demonstrating God's reign over the universe and the forces of nature that the Egyptians idolized), Moses led Israel out of Egypt and into the desert. It was in the desert that God set the foundation for his kingdom through Israel by creating a covenant with them. The culminating moment of the coming of the kingdom was when God gave Moses the covenant stipulations (Ten Commandments); this moment was followed by God's *taking up residence* in the Tabernacle. While they were in the desert, the Tabernacle would be the place from where God would reign over and through his people in holiness and righteousness. God's plan was that through Israel's faithful obedience to the Torah, God would reign over the nations through his covenant people.

This, in a breath, is the story of the exodus (and the wilderness wandering)—first rebellion and deliverance, then kingdom. We cannot miss the fact that the goal of the exodus is for God to share his holy reign and presence among his people. The first exodus is a type of the one to come about through the messianic king.[5]

Why Two Exoduses?

But why do we need two exoduses? Isn't one adequate? The answer lies in the tragedy of Israel's story. The story of Israel, which is fulfilled in Jesus, indicates quite clearly that God, in his righteousness, wisdom, and faithfulness, is willing to put himself in a position where his plans are deeply impacted by human choice. More than this, what Israel could not accomplish

4. This is also true of Jesus, as noted in the previous chapter. Jesus' miracles not only reveal the nature of God, but the fact that God has authorized him as the expected deliverer.

5. For an excellent and more thorough treatment of the exodus as a type of New Testament salvation, see Oswalt, *Exodus*.

as the chosen family of God, Jesus accomplishes as the True Israel (see chapter 3), through his sonship.

Interestingly enough, God predicted Israel's infidelity and disobedience to the Torah well before it happened. We read this in Deuteronomy 31:16, 20, and 29:

> And the LORD said to Moses, "Behold, you are about to lie down with your fathers. Then this people will rise and whore after the foreign gods among them in the land that they are entering, and *they will forsake me and break my covenant that I have made with them* (Exod 31:16; emphasis added).

> For when I have brought them into the land flowing with milk and honey, which I swore to give to their fathers, and they have eaten and are full and grown fat, *they will turn to other gods and serve them, and despise me and break my covenant* (Exod 31:2; emphasis added).

> For I know that after my death you will surely act corruptly and turn aside from the way that I have commanded you. And in the days to come evil will befall you, because you will do what is evil in the sight of the Lord, provoking him to anger through the work of your hands (Exod 31:29).

Even though Moses was not a king like David, he was a national leader for God's people. In fact, Moses is arguably the *most important* national-leader of God's people. This meant that the Messiah would not only be like David in his royalty, but he would also be like Moses in his role as *deliverer* from the evil powers of the world personified in Pharaoh and Egypt in the first exodus. So, once again, in the Messiah we have the telescoping of a deliverance (Mosaic exodus) that would result in a global Jewish empire (Davidic king). This is what the Messiah was expected to accomplish in his Davidic and Mosaic roles.

The New Testament understands the messianic events (cross, resurrection, and Pentecost) this way. The NT understands that what happened centuries before in the Israelite deliverance from Egypt echoes Christ's work on the cross. Even Jesus himself makes reference to this when he says, "For if you believed Moses, you would believe me; for he wrote of me" (John 5:46). Jesus is referring to the passage in Deuteronomy where Moses says, "The LORD your God will raise up for you a prophet like me from among you, from your brothers—it is to him you shall listen" (Deut 18:15).

The Exodus and Propitiation

The exodus in the Old Testament was the high moment of salvation for the family of Abraham, the people of God. It is the exodus that subsequent generations look back to as the culminating moment of the national Hebrew identity. It is the event in which their transcendent and holy God broke into history and delivered them. This is their testimony. It is in the exodus that God made the nation of Israel a people of his own possession (Ps 114:1).

At the center of that event, interestingly enough, *very little is said about the forgiveness of sins*. It is the sacrificial system that is established at Sinai that brings atonement into the dialogue as a key element of the covenant code. Obviously, the sacrificial system didn't come until the establishment of the Mosaic law at Sinai *after* deliverance under Pharaoh. Nonetheless, to talk about forgiveness of sins at the event of the exodus would be anachronistic. This is a strong indicator in itself that God's World Renewal Plan is about much more than atonement. We must adjust our theology in light of the fact that the cross (like the exodus) is not *merely* about substitutionary atonement; we must arrive at the place in our thinking where we understand that forgiveness of sins is a *means for the establishment of God's holy reign on earth*. Kingdom is the endgame.

Passover

Let us consider the Passover event for a moment. The Passover, as the pivotal event in the sequence of liberation miracles, does indeed point to atonement for sin. However, even in the Passover narrative itself (Exod 12), very little is mentioned concerning the forgiveness of sins beyond the symbol of the sacrificial lamb, and even then, the sacrificial lamb is situated in a much larger context where there is quite a lot of other things happening regarding Israel's redemption. The blood of the lamb being on the doorpost would cause the angel of death to "pass over" the house. Victor Hamilton helpfully goes into detail on the various nuances of the tri-consonantal Hebrew root *p-s-q*. He concludes that "stand/stood watch over" is a better translation than "passover."[6] This means that we should not only visualize the Destroyer "passing over" Hebrew homes, but the Destroyer passing over Hebrew homes *because this is where God stood watch*. Hamilton writes, "The God of Exod. 12 . . . [as a] . . . protecting God for those inside, behind

---

6. Hamilton, *Exodus*, 185.

the blood. Because, and only because, the Lord will stand watch over his people, a 'Destroyer' will not be able to enter their houses."[7]

So where does forgiveness for sins correlate with deliverance? Exegetically speaking, the concept seems to hardly enter the picture. While we can legitimately read *back into the story elements of atonement*, one is hard-pressed to find it here. After all, the Egyptian slavery is not punishment for sin as the Exile was. So, while the Passover meal certainly can represent the forgiveness of sins *later* on in light of the sacrificial system (in particular connection with the Day of Atonement), it also represents something greater: *God's power to save his people from death*. While the firstborn sons of Egypt are dying all around, it is the people of Israel who are saved. The Passover narrative tells us that through participating in blood sacrifice God's people can be saved from his judgment. The deliverance of Israel from Egypt, the giving of the Torah and the gift of the Promised Land *all serve the purpose of God establishing his reign on earth through his covenant people.*

Traditionally, then, when reading New Testament salvation back into the exodus as a type of deliverance to come, the Passover is the atoning event. Paired with this is the crossing of the Red Sea, which is a type of resurrection, and the giving of the covenant at Sinai, which is a type of Pentecost.

This is what is behind Paul speaking of Jesus as the Passover lamb when he says, "For Christ, our Passover lamb, has been sacrificed. Let us therefore celebrate the festival, not with the old leaven, the leaven of malice and evil, but with the unleavened bread of sincerity and truth" (1 Cor 5:7–8). Here, Paul makes the political and theological inseparable. The exodus is a political deliverance from Egypt, and the cross is a deliverance from all the powers that be in the world from Caesar and Rome to the Adversary and the forces of evil.

This is all to say that yes, at the *center* of the work of Jesus on the cross is the work of substitutionary atonement. However, this work serves a greater purpose that goes beyond the forgiveness of sins. What is that greater purpose? That greater purpose is the establishment of the rule and reign of God on earth. Through the cross, Jesus overthrows the powers of sin and death that run parallel with the Pharaoh of the first exodus. With the resurrection in sight, the reign of sin and death is dethroned and Jesus takes his place of authority as the king.

7. Ibid.

If the cross is the second exodus, then Jesus, as mentioned above, is the second Moses. This is a theme that we see running throughout the life of Jesus as we have it according to the canonical Gospels. Jesus is presented as the second Moses primarily as a covenant-maker. The dynamics of Jesus as covenant-maker are explained in detail in chapter two. However, let's briefly touch on the various ways that Jesus is the covenant-maker and giver of the law, just as Moses was.

Jesus as the Second Moses

Matthew's gospel is the clearest on presenting Jesus as the second Moses. This makes perfect sense in that it is clear from clues in the text that Matthew writes to a primarily Jewish audience. This means that he is presenting Jesus within a Jewish theological and eschatological framework.

One of the ways that Matthew highlights this is by arranging Jesus' teaching into five discourses.[8] This five-part arrangement is intended to echo the five-part structure of the Torah. This is accentuated even further through the fact that two of the five discourses are give from mountaintops (the Sermon on the Mount and the Mount Olivet Discourse), just as Moses delivered the Torah from the top of a mountain (Sinai). Further still, the content of each discourse is teaching and commentary on the Torah itself. The Sermon on the Mount, the first discourse, fits this description best. In the Sermon on the Mount, Jesus regularly uses the formula, "You have heard it said . . . but I say to you . . ." In other words, Jesus is making himself equal with Moses by adding to the Mosaic law.

Another exodus dimension of Jesus' calling is accentuated with the triumphal entry of Jesus into Jerusalem (Matt 21). It was precisely at the time of the Passover festival, which celebrates the remembrance of the exodus, that Jesus went to the cross. As Jesus entered Jerusalem, the crowd celebrated with loud voice and deed as they waved palm branches and shouted, "Hosanna to the Son of David! Blessed is he who comes in the name of the Lord! Hosanna in the highest!" (Matt 21:9) This comes right from Psalm 118:25–26. Psalm 118 is the last of six psalms (113–118) known as the *Egyptian Hallel*. The *Egyptian Hallel* was (and is) sung to commemorate Passover in the Jewish tradition.[9] The famous Last Supper (*Seder*) was

8. See Keener, *Gospel of Matthew*, 36.

9. Psalms 113 and 114 are sung before the Passover meal and Psalm 115–118 after the meal. Cf. De Claissé-Walford et al., *Book of Psalms*, 847.

the Passover meal just before Jesus, as the new Passover lamb, went to the cross. This means that Jesus is coming into Jerusalem to be handed over to the authorities at the very moment of Passover. The people who celebrated Jesus' arrival had a dual expectation from their leader. First, they expected the Messiah to lead rebellion against Rome, just as Moses did. Second, they hoped that the rebellion would result in the establishment of a global, Jewish empire.

The hopes of the people were high. After all, Jesus demonstrated his miraculous power for three years. This demonstration of power testified to his messianic anointing. It's no surprise, then, when just hours after praising him, they shout, "Crucify him!" (Matt 27:22) as Jesus appears weak and silent before Pilate, their great Roman foe. Where are his powers now?

As Jesus is handed over to worldly powers personified in the human arrogance of Rome and its leaders, the lamb is led to the slaughter. It is through the sacrifice of one that the nation would be saved. Herein lies the irony of the words of Caiaphas, the High Priest (John 18:14). The sacrifice of the Passover lamb in the exodus always pointed to Jesus, the sacrifice through which the wrath of God is appeased (propitiation), sinners are forgiven (expiation), and God's people are liberated from slavery to the powers of this world. In light of the exodus, the cross is the moment of deliverance.

We cannot overlook at this very point that the cross as the second exodus is the *means for the establishment of a new covenant, and a new covenant people.* This is the coming kingdom that Israel had been waiting for. While the propitiatory function of the cross is a part of this, the *thrust* of the semantic value of the cross is *the coming kingdom* when we interpret it properly in its historical context as the second exodus.

Another place where this same principle comes to the surface is in John 6. This is the "I am the bread of life" chapter. Jesus, in teaching that he himself is the bread of life, makes a strong connection between bread of life and eternal life. He also has quite a bit to say about the Father drawing people to himself for salvation. How do these three themes, motifs, relate to one another? First let's define what Jesus means in each motif, and then we will show how they relate to one another.

1. I am the bread of life. Here, Jesus is saying that he alone can satisfy the deeper, everlasting hunger pangs of humanity. There is no food that keeps us full and satisfied forever. Each time we eat or drink, our hunger and thirst (human needs) are satisfied, but then, after a short time, our bellies begin to grumble, and our mouths become parched. Jesus draws on this

truth of human existence to form an analogy in order to teach that he is the ultimate solution to human need. In a nutshell, *Jesus is saying that he can reverse death*. This is the great tragedy of human existence that no one in human history has been able to undo. This is where Jesus' "I am the resurrection and the life" comes in as well.

2. Eternal Life. Surprisingly, there is quite a lot of debate over what this term means in the New Testament. "Eternal Life" truly is a misnomer when applied to humanity. The proper term is "everlasting life" because "eternal" means without beginning and without end, and because human are created beings, they are not without a beginning. All created beings came into existence at a particular point in history. Jesus, by way of contrast, was eternally preexistent (see John 1). So, what Jesus is *not* saying here is that people who believe in him and eat of his flesh will somehow become eternally preexistent. What he *is* saying is that those who eat of his flesh and believe in him will be released from the chains of death; life with beginning, yet without end.

Finally, eating Jesus' flesh and drinking his blood is a symbol. We realize this when we read the story of the Last Supper. It is a symbol of receiving the gift of saving faith in Jesus, and most importantly, faith in his death as an effective atoning sacrifice for believers. Receiving this gift makes individuals become members of God's covenant people. In turn this means that believers receive the heritage of Abraham who was delivered from the curse of death through the gift of a son (Isaac). We are God's covenant people who inherit the gift of life everlasting.

3. The Father Draws People to Jesus. It is in this motif that motif 1 (I am the bread of life) begins to gain further clarity still. Jesus saying that he is the bread of life is quite a lofty statement, as the Jews in the passage recognize and grumble about (John 6:41). I would have been grumbling too if I heard some guy going around saying that he had the key to all life's problems and he could undo the problem of death if people would simply eat his flesh and drink his blood. This is such a bizarre statement that *the confirming testimony of the Holy Spirit is the only way anyone can take this claim seriously*. This is always the case with the truth of the Gospel. And this is why salvation is always *only* the work of the Holy Spirit. There is not nearly enough moral excellence or human capacity to be able to either identify or choose the gospel in separation from grace and the Holy Spirit.[10] When we look

---

10. This is where John Wesley's doctrine of prevenient grace comes in. It is the grace

upon the story of God in the cross and the resurrection with human eyes without the testimony of the Holy Spirit, we see only folly and foolishness.

So, to believe in Jesus' words here that we must eat his flesh and drink his blood (which is a symbol for intimate and deep faith in his death as the means for God's new covenant people) requires divine intervention in the human mind and will. This is only possible because of grace.

So, how do these fit together? We have begun to see it a bit already. Here's how it works: all of humanity is faced with the tragic need of deliverance from death. Jesus and Jesus alone can resolve this issue. The issue is resolved through faith in his death. Not just any faith, but a faith that is a gracious gift from heaven. Receiving this faith makes believers members of God's covenant people, defined by their saving faith in the death and resurrection of the Jewish Messiah who died both for the Jews and for the world. The symbol for a public demonstration of saving faith in Jesus is the Lord's Supper, the place where the bread and wine symbolize the flesh and blood of Jesus broken and shed on the cross for the world.

So, in a sentence, Jesus alone saves and this seems foolish, which is why anyone who embraces this is a product of the work of the Holy Spirit, not human effort or logic.

This means that every part of the redemption story hinges on the cross. The cross stands at the center of God's World Renewal Plan. Everything prior to the cross leads to the cross, and everything subsequent to the cross flows from the cross. The mission of God to reestablish his reign on earth with humanity as his image bearers and representatives, is fulfilled through the cross. From the very start of the story, God's promise was *for* a people, *through* a people. The reign of God that was lost in the garden is reestablished through the cross. The kingdom of God is reestablished through the obedient death of Jesus. Jesus the Messiah, through his unwavering obedience and servanthood, fulfills that which Israel as a nation could not.

Jesus is the True Israel. The nation of Israel was intended to be the means of blessing for the nations. It was God's intention all along that that through Israel all would experience and witness the redemptive work of God. It was intended that through Israel God's reign would overthrow the reign of sin and death and bring life and blessing to the world. Beale sums it up with this, "The New Testament pictures Christ and the church as finally

---

that "goes before" that gives the Holy Spirit room to share his testimony about Jesus as the bread of life to prospective believers. Not only this, but the idea that there is no human capacity to save oneself is the doctrine of total depravity.

having done what Adam, Noah, and Israel had failed to do in extending the temple of God's presence throughout the world."[11]

In the cross, Jesus puts an end to the powers of the world personified in the Roman cross. Tom Thatcher says, "Indeed, in the Fourth Gospel the normal meaning of the Cross is profaned in a way that makes Caesar and his agents helpless victims of the Christ who conquered the world (John 16:33)."[12] Thatcher expands the idea with this:

> In John's world, crucifixion was not only a messy and expensive way to dispatch with undesirable people, but also, and much more significantly, a bookmark in the fable of Roman power. Every Cross told a story; every story has a moral; the moral of the Cross story was calculated to rationalize and maintain the imperial status quo. To explore the story inscribed in the Cross, it will be helpful to briefly review Yael Zerubavel's discussion of the "commemorative narratives" that undergird a society's public rituals, and also Michael Foucault's model of "countermemory." Taken together, these approaches offer a reading strategy that exposes both the values latent in Roman crucifixions and John's attempt to reverse those values in his presentation of Christ's death.[13]

Once again, the emphasis here is that in the cross we have the very moment in which power is transferred from the fallen world to Jesus. The cross is the culminating moment of kingship for Jesus as the Messiah as he actively turns the earthly empire on its head and takes back what was his to begin with. This is precisely why submission is so crucial in the midst of this recapitulation. Through force and might the world exercises and exerts its governance. Through submission, obedience, and love, Christ the king establishes the true kingdom as it was always meant to be.

We cannot miss yet another important second exodus dimension of Jesus' life and that is the Last Supper. In all four of the Gospels we find the narrative of the Last Supper (thereby highlighting its importance). This is where Jesus partook in the *Seder* meal with his disciples not only to celebrate Passover, but also to establish the new covenant. It is in this event that Jesus clearly identifies himself not only with Moses as the covenant maker, but as the actual Passover Lamb. "Take, eat; this is my body" (Matt 26:26). As it was ritual to eat the sacrificial lamb that was the means to their

---

11. Beale, *Temple and the Church's Mission*, 169.

12. Thatcher, "'I have conquered the world,'" 140.

13. Ibid, 143.

deliverance from death, they now ate the bread (*maṣāh*) as a symbol of Christ's flesh. So, once again, Jesus not only makes the covenant, but also offers himself as the sacrifice that seals the covenant. Once again, more has been said on this already in chapter two.

Second Exodus: Conclusion

It becomes clear through these features of the Gospels that Jesus is to be understood as the second Moses and the cross as the second exodus. The cross, then, is a symbol of the new covenant blood. The blood of this covenant, however, was different than the blood of animals. The writer of Hebrews says,

> For since the law has but a shadow of the good things to come instead of the true form of these realities, it can never, by the same sacrifices that are continually offered every year, make perfect those who draw near. Otherwise, would they have ceased to be offered, since the worshipers, having once been cleansed, would no longer have any consciousness of sins? But in these sacrifices there is a reminder of sins every year. For it is impossible for the blood of bulls and goats to take away sins (Heb 10:1–4).

But how does the cross as the second exodus relate to salvation and holiness? To answer this question let's look at the connection with justification and the faithfulness of God.

Justification, the Faithfulness of God, and the New Covenant

We find in the sacrificial system a means for dealing with the ongoing problem of sin-guilt. God, as a holy, pure, and just being, cannot dwell with impurity. He is set apart; he is different than the created order. Going beyond this still, his own character is set apart from the fallen character of humanity. God is set apart in two senses First, he is set apart in that he's not restricted by time and space and nothing in the created order can properly represent him. Unlike the creation, he is not dependent on any other. This is one of the many interpretations for the divine name, "YAHWEH." John Oswalt says this:

What else is Yahweh saying about himself when he introduces himself to Moses as I AM? He is saying that he is totally self-existent. He is dependent on nothing and no one else. Only one being in the universe can say that, because every other being is dependent on that one.[14]

In this way, God is *different*.

In another sense, he is different from humanity in his ethics. He is good. Unlike humanity, he doesn't steal, cheat, lie, betray, or hate. He is honest, faithful, gracious, good, just, righteous, and loving. He is *holy*. While humanity is impure in its ethics, God is perfectly clean and without reproach.

With this, God uses the Torah to communicate this reality to Israel. Israel must understand that God is different, he is apart, he is holy. What better way to teach this to Israel than to have them ask before each meal, "Is this food clean or unclean?" Or ask at the end of each day, "Is tomorrow holy or not?" Or even question the clothes they put on, "Is this pure or impure?" The Torah penetrates every dimension of human life and activity in order to thrust the message forward that God is *holy and righteous*.

Food laws, the Sabbath, dress codes, and other Torah commands aren't the only object lessons that teach the holiness of YAHWEH. We also find the sacrificial system. The sacrificial system provided a means by which God could solve the ongoing sin-guilt problem of Israel. Not only this, but the sacrificial system also created a means by which God could manifest his heavenly reign on earth. *Because of the sacrificial system that created a means for propitiation and expiation for sin, heaven was able come down by grace and fill the temple.* This is the image that we find when God's glory fills the tabernacle in the desert following the exodus. This is the image that Ezekiel the prophet sees in exile—the return of the glory of God, the return of God's reign on earth through his elect human agents. Tragically (at least it's tragic for a moment, then Christ redeems the tragedy through the cross and resurrection), Israel cannot help but violate the covenant. It is because of Israel's disobedience that God's reign on earth through his chosen people is once again thwarted (first in the Garden, then with Noah, now with Israel).[15]

Israel's inability to obey the Torah and consequent failure to embody God's reign on earth resulted in not only exile, but also the *promise of a*

---

14. Oswalt, *Exodus*, 45.

15. There's also the case of David's murder and adultery that can be added to this list.

new covenant. The Sinai covenant was external. It was a list of external rules explaining how to behave. The purpose of the law was to oversee, manage and guide the behavior of Israel so that their status as God's people could be maintained (not so that they could be saved, as the exodus had already occurred). Through Israel's failure *via* the violation of the Torah and covenant, we learn that the problem is not external but *internal.* It is a *heart* problem, not a body problem. This does not mean that there is no problem with the body. To the contrary, it is in the physical world that the spiritual problem precisely manifests that "the wages of sin is death" (Rom 6:23).

Because the Mosaic law is unable to undo the penalty of death because of its inability to induce internal, spiritual transformation and rebirth, there arises the need for a new covenant. The purpose of the new covenant, according to the prophets, is to facilitate a *heart change* that results in true deliverance from the power of sin and death (cf. Jer 31:31–34). This heart change would come about through the forgiveness of sins (Jer 31:34 and Ezek 36:25–27). This means that it is through *the justification of sinners* that God's World Renewal Project can be fulfilled.

The New Perspective on Imputed Righteousness

There is a great deal of debate on the issue of justification of believers through the cross. Much ink has been spilt over this and there is no need, therefore, to detail it all out here.[16] However, let's simply say that the NP has made a case against the Reformed doctrine of imputed righteousness. The doctrine of imputed righteousness essentially states that the righteousness that is Christ's is given to, or placed upon, the believer in the moment of faith. The NP argues that this is not what Paul taught in his letters. They argue that in the courtroom metaphor, when the judge declares the accused "not guilty," he does not transfer his own righteousness to the accused. Rather, in the case of the believer in Jesus' Christ as Lord and Savior, the judge declares the accused "not guilty" simply because Jesus has made due payment in the place of the accused. There is no need to transfer Jesus' or anyone else's righteousness to the believer. Rather, the faithfulness of Jesus to God the Father has allowed for an efficacious substitutionary atonement that allows for believers to be declared innocent. This variation of understanding justification means that the old way of thinking that when God looks at the believer he sees Jesus is

16. See Wright, *Justification* for a detailed account of the debate as well as the NP's interpretive response to the Reformed tradition.

misleading. When God the Father, or anyone else, looks at the believer, they see the believer who was guilty but has been *declared innocent* because of his faith in Jesus and his atoning work.

Internal Cleansing

So how do we interpret this in light of the fulfillment of the Mosaic law? We said before that Torah observance was unable to alleviate the problem of death as the consequence of sin. The Mosaic law is unable to provide the transformation of the heart and rebirth that is required for redemption from the wages of sin. The righteous death of Jesus, however, makes powerful payment with blood unlike that of bulls, rams, lamb, sheep, or any other animal, and allows for the life of Christ to be made one with the life of the believer. Jesus' blood allows for *an internal cleansing* that the Torah was unable to accomplish.

This feature of the Gospel is very much present in the story of the wedding at Cana (John 2). In that story, Jesus is invited (along with this disciples and mother) to a wedding. During the wedding celebration the host runs out of wine. Mary looks to Jesus to resolve this problem. Jesus says to Mary, "Woman, what does this have to do with me? My hour has not yet come." Jesus is saying that he's come to die and rise again, not to make provision for a wedding feast. At the same time, the wedding feast is analogous to his redemptive work on the cross. The redemption of the believer culminates in a sort of wedding feast where the church and Christ come together to celebrate the wondrous union for which God has made provision. This is why, even though Jesus resists, he goes ahead and responds to Mary's request.

Jesus instructs the servants to "Fill the jars with water" (John 2:7); but what kind of jars? These jars are jars used for the *external purification*. The Jews used these jars to hold water used for ceremonial washing. All impurity would be washed away and the believer would be made ceremonially clean when water was drawn from these jars. This time it is not water that will be taken from these jars; this time, wine will be consumed from these jars. The object lesson here is that this wine that is consumed can cleanse *internally*. This wine not only cleanses the believer from the guilt and impurity that is accumulated from sinning, but also cures the guilt of the *sin nature* that is seated at the heart of men. This wine links up with the wine of the new covenant that we read about when Jesus celebrates Passover with his disciples (1 Cor 11:25). This is the wine that when consumed will cause an internal heart change and transformation that will allow for new life. This wine is the blood of Christ that gives everlasting life. This wine will consume the believer.

This demonstrates once again that the problem with humanity is *internal*. The problem is the human heart. It is the heart that needs cleansing; this very internal cleansing is the image that the wine offers us. This is the cleansing that Jesus offers. John Oswalt recalls the symbol of leaven for sin. Oswalt writes this:

> Over and over again, leaven is the symbol for sin. Like leaven, sin cannot be confined to a small part of our lives; very shortly, it contaminates the whole. Like leaven, sin will take the natural, fresh elements of life and ferment them. Like leaven, sin promotes decay and ultimate leads to death.[17]

What's needed is something that goes beyond the forgiveness of sins. What's needed is a new nature—a new creation. This new creation is delivered within the framework of a new covenant. We will treat this in further detail in the next chapter.

With this we can see how the cross, atonement, the new covenant, and the second exodus all come together. The cross, once again, isn't the place where all that we receive is the forgiveness of sins. No, the cross is the place where we receive the forgiveness of sins, internal cleansing, and the new covenant through which God's reign can manifest on earth. There is a new place, however, from which God will reign. In the Old Testament, for the covenant made at Sinai, God reigned from the Tabernacle and the Temple; now, it is *the believer* who is the Temple of God. We will explore this concept further in the next chapter.

The Twist: Death on a Roman Cross?

The Gospels make it clear that even though the Old Testament prepared for the fulfillment of God's World Renewal Plan something must have gone wrong if the Messiah ended up on a Roman cross, right? What people didn't expect was for the kingdom of God to be *launched through the suffering, death, and resurrection of the king*. This dimension of the kingdom and the king only made sense after Pentecost. It was when believers had

17. Oswalt, *Exodus*, 99.

the illumination of the Holy Spirit that they understood what the kingdom was all about and how it was through the cross alone that the kingdom could come in its fullness. They also understood that it was through Jesus' weakness and submission that his power and authority over the earth as the rightful king was established. Finally, through the witness of the resurrected body of Christ, they understood that the kingdom would be more than just any kingdom; it would also be a new creation. In Jesus, God became king, launched his kingdom on earth, as well as the New Creation. The end of God's World Renewal Plan had begun.

5

Kingdom

*The New Creation, the Faithfulness of God,
and Holiness*

Thoughts about myself hinder my usefulness to God. God is not after perfecting me to be a specimen in His show-room; He is getting me to the place where He can use me. Let Him do what He likes.

—OSWALD CHAMBERS[1]

IN THE PREVIOUS CHAPTER, we explored the death of Jesus as the means through which the new covenant is established. We said that in the cross we find not only a means for the atonement for sin, but also the means through which God's reign would be reestablished on earth and his World Renewal Plan fulfilled. We said that this was precisely the purpose of atonement for sin-guilt. We also saw that the exodus was a type of messianic event in that it was the redemptive event that led to God's reign in and through his people. Furthermore, we said that Moses was a type of Christ in that he was an intermediary covenant-maker between God and the chosen people of God. In the same way that Moses functioned as God's chosen servant to lead a rebellion against the oppressive reign of Pharaoh, Jesus functions as God's chosen servant who leads the great rebellion against the oppressive reign of sin and death over not only Israel, but over all the *cosmos*.

---

1. Chambers, *My Utmost for His Highest*, Dec. 2.

In this chapter we will go further by concluding our study with an exploration of the kingdom of God and how it fits within the bigger picture of God's World Renewal Plan. We will see that when all the dimensions of Christology, soteriology, ecclesiology, and eschatology merge together in the kingdom of God we gain a clear and fresh perspective of salvation. We will see that the glory of God that descended on the Tabernacle in Exodus 40 is a type of Pentecost. Just as the Passover isn't solely for the purpose of deliverance from Egypt, so the cross is not *solely* for the purpose of atoning for sin-guilt. Both of these (the Passover and the cross) are a means for God's coming glory. *God delivered Israel from Egypt so that they would become his holy nation, his nation of priests through whom the effects of the garden would be reversed.* In the Garden humanity took upon itself moral autonomy thereby corrupting the vocational dimension of the image of God. Jesus recapitulates this failure through his perfect obedience and servanthood. Through expressed faith in the Lordship of Jesus, believers submit once again to the reign of God by means of the Holy Spirit that recreates the heart of humanity for servanthood, humility, trust, and complete obedience according to the Spirit of Jesus the king. In this feature of the cross, the role of servanthood and perfect obedience comes to light. With the character of humanity conforming to the perfect obedience of the Messiah, the image of God once again is restored in humanity and his righteous, good, just, and loving reign is reestablished on the earth.

What about the resurrection? We will see that God's solution all along was to redeem the corruption and decay of the physical order by *recreating* the *cosmos*. This means that the kingdom of God is not only a spiritual reality, it is also a physical reality. This is modeled in the glorified body of Christ. We will see that the resurrection of Jesus has nothing to do with dying and going to heaven. Rather, it has everything to do with the fact that right in the middle of history, God has launched his new creation through the resurrection of his obedient Son and all that conform to him by faith will also be conformed to him in a future resurrection.

To finish, we will see that salvation comes into fresh perspective in a number of ways when reading the New Testament with the adjusted, NP lens. We will see that salvation and holiness is about a devoted heart, yes. We will also see that the outpouring of that devoted heart is a posture of *vocational servanthood*. We will also consider the link between salvation and God's reign over the corporate, covenant people of God. Furthermore, we will see that salvation and holiness is not all about the state of *my heart*, but the state of corporate church that collectively testifies to the triune image of God through vocation.

Flames of Fire: A Holy Calling

For a long time I interpreted the flames of fire at Pentecost as a heart change. There's no doubt that this is the case, however, is there another level of interpretation to these long-awaited flames? For Moses, the flame that burned in the bush chose him for a mission. God's indwelling cleanses us and his indwelling and abiding presence executes the circumcision of the heart. It is Christ's work that makes that possible. At the same time we must ask, *for what purpose does he cleanse us?* Does he clean us simply for the sake of being clean, or is our sanctification and indwelling of his glory serve a greater purpose? *I believe that he cleanses us so that we can be useful vessels through which his redemptive power can flow.*

We see this in the vision and commission of the prophet in Isaiah 6. In this chapter we read about the prophet's vision of YAHWEH who is seated on his throne, high and lifted up, and whose robe's train fills the temple. This is a powerful God. The first verse of the chapter details for us that Isaiah sees this vision in the year that King Uzziah died. Uzziah was a powerful man. We have two kings mentioned in these first few verses of Isaiah 6: (1) Uzziah and (2) YAHWEH. One of these kings is dead and the other is very much alive. What's ironic about this is that the people of Judah tremble in fear because their human king is dead. It's laughable. They only fear because they overlook the fact that the One who really matters is alive and well and in their midst, overseeing the affairs of human history and directing the outcome of events (reminds you a bit of the story of the disciples panicking because of the storm on the boat. All the while, Jesus is with them, full of power).

Not only is this the most powerful God (symbolized in the train of his robe and being seated on a high throne), but also he's also incomparably holy. The trifold repetition of a Hebrew adjective demonstrates a superlative. This God of Israel is *The* Holy One. There is none who is more holy. This is a dangerous combination: *powerful* and *holy*. This means that he can destroy any impure being that enters his presence. His holiness even surpasses that of the *seraphim* (which literally means "burning ones" in Hebrew). What is more pure than fire? And here stands poor Isaiah, the man of unclean lips living among a people of unclean lips. He is undone! For Isaiah death is imminent.

Rather than destroying Isaiah, however, God purifies him. He forgives his sins. Here we see that cleanliness is a metaphor for innocence. This means that impurity symbolizes guilt, namely, sin-guilt; back to this in a moment. But why does God forgive Isaiah? First and foremost, he does this because he is a loving and merciful God. This is a part of his holiness. This is a part of his character. The second reason for Isaiah's cleansing *is that God has a job for Isaiah.* What is so fascinating about this passage is that God doesn't say, "Okay, Isaiah, I've cleaned your lips, now you go and be my mouthpiece." Rather, what God says is, "I need someone to send, who will go?" In other words, he forgives Isaiah, and *then extends an invitation;* much to our surprise, Isaiah volunteers. Isaiah goes from cowering in front of the all powerful, mighty, and holy God to jumping up and down, hand in the air, volunteering for service. This is a mighty heart change! This chance has come about as a result of the purifying fire.

With this, we see that *our heart change is for a purpose. God transforms our hearts for vocational purposes. We must go beyond talking about having a fully devoted heart to having a fully missional lifestyle when we talk about salvation and holiness.* This is our number one feature of salvation in fresh perspective. Once again, the cross is the best example of this. In the cross, yes, we see the heart posture of a loving God towards his people, but we *also see the fulfillment of the mission of God and that the very impetus for that mission is his holy heart.*

This text from Isaiah reminds us yet again that we do great damage to the meaning of the text when we cannot separate the New Testament from its Old Testament theological heritage. Continually in the Old Testament, God the Father sends the Holy Spirit for the sake of fulfilling a God-given commission. Undoubtedly, there are also ontological features of the pouring out of the Holy Spirit in the Old Testament; however, those features are always framed for eschatalogical and missional purposes. In particular, the peace that will come because of the Holy Spirit being poured out on believers is connected with the coming of the messianic rule and reign and the universal establishment of the kingdom of God on earth.

Continuing Christ's Work

Kingdom building is not something that is done in human strength. Kingdom building is done through participation with Christ in bringing healing dynamics of the indwelling of the Holy Spirit to the world. It is the Holy Spirit who *continues* the work of Christ through believers. It is this Spirit-presence dimension of vocation that makes this entire concept *different* from the liberal social gospel. This is something very different than that. This is God's eternal work; the work that is continuous with the New Creation that was launched in the bodily resurrection of Jesus. It is also discontinuous with the present evil age. In other words, it is not the job of humanity to go on building God's kingdom solely through the infusion of Judeo-Christian ideals in the postmodern political arena. Kingdom building means bringing healing to the broken and decaying world by the power, compassion, and love of King Jesus through the Holy Spirit—to bring the light of the kingdom into the place of darkness and isolation.

We see this sort of activity in the book of Acts as the early Christians participated in continuing Christ's work after Pentecost. What the apostles were doing was not infiltrating Roman government, running for office, or leading political rebellions in the name of Jesus. No, they were proclaiming a message of hope and healing in the Jewish Messiah. Indeed, Paul announces that it is Jesus who reigns, and not Caesar (Rom 1:1–4); however, this is a cosmic claim more than a political one. This is Paul saying that God has retaken the throne of his creation once again and his work is the result of his faithfulness to Israel. Paul and the rest of the apostles were preaching that the New Creation has come in Jesus; that the end of the story has come bursting into the present and now people can live in this new reality based on the forgiveness of sins and commissioned with a call to godly stewardship. This is holiness, both sins forgiven and the vocation of humanity properly restored in Jesus.

Pentecost and Kābôd Elohim

Pentecost is the Jewish celebration of the giving of the Torah fifty days after Passover. Pentecost as a messianic event reminds us that it is through God's chosen people that the Creator's redemption will come to the *cosmos*. Once God gets Israel out of Egypt, he instructs them to build the Tabernacle so that he may take up residence among them. Once they do this, the *kābôd* ĕlōhîm ("glory of God") comes down and dwells in the Tabernacle in the midst of Israel. This is the purpose of the exodus.

What's interesting here is that the phrases "presence of God" and "glory of God" are interchangeable in this passage (Exod 40:34). What's fascinating about this is that this is the moment that the creation, just for a period, returns to the place of its original design. The creation exists to glorify the Creator. This happens when the image of God is properly functioning in humanity as originally intended by YAHWEH. When humanity fails to reflect the glory of God into the creation and simultaneously reflect worship back up to the Creator, then everything is out of order; chaos reigns. In this moment, once everything in the Tabernacle is properly purified and prepared for the all holy presence of God, God's glory returns.

We cannot miss the connection between the atoning sacrifices and the glory of God returning to the face of the earth. These are essential because of the *holiness of God*. Without these, God is just like all the other gods of the ancient Near Eastern pantheon—created in the image of humanity. But this is not what we have here in the story of the exodus or in the story of Pentecost. In both of these accounts, a proper atoning work must take place. Humanity must be prepared. *Expiation* must occur. There must be a cleansing from sin-guilt *in order for* God's presence, and thereby his glory, to return.

For this to happen there must be a turning away from sin. In particular, there must be a turning away from the will to be morally autonomous. To sum this up in one word: there is a need for *servanthood*. We must forfeit the heart-posture that is plagued with pride and ego and let God be God. We must submit. This is what N. T. Wright means when he says, "And at the heart of both parts of this tension stands the cross of the Messiah, at once the long-awaited fulfillment and the slap in the face for all human pride."[2] This is precisely what Jesus is talking about when he says, "come to me, all who labor and are heavy laden, and I will give you rest. Take my yoke upon you, and learn from me, for I am gentle and lowly in heart, and you will find rest for your souls. For my yoke is easy, and my burden is light" (Matt 11:28–30). Jesus is saying, "Stop trying to be the God of your life. Let me be God in your life. My burden is much easier."

It almost seems as if Jesus is being contradictory with this passage because on the one hand he says things like, "take up your cross and follow me" (Matt 16:24). What we often miss in this, however, is that just before

2. Wright, *Paul in Fresh Perspective*, 54.

he says this he says, "If anyone would came after me, *let him deny himself* and take up his cross and follow me" (emphasis added). This harmonizes perfectly with Jesus' promise that his burden is light. Again, what he is saying is that life will be what it was intended if you give up being God in your own life, if you submit the moral autonomy that was never meant for you but always meant for God. Allow God to decide what is good and what is not good. Give up deciding on your own, for he will make his will known to you through the indwelling of the Holy Spirit. All of this, every bit of it, requires repentance, requires turning away from moral autonomy and turning towards God. It means servanthood and alleviation from sin-guilt. Once this happens, then his very glory can come down and dwell in our midst.

C. S. Lewis describes this reality this way:

> Give up yourself, and you will find your real self. Lose your life and you will save it. Submit to death, the death of your ambitions and favorite wishes every day and the death of your whole body in the end: Submit with every fiber of your being, and you will find eternal life. Keep back nothing. Nothing that you have not given away will be really yours. Nothing in you that has not died will ever be raised from the dead. Look for yourself, and you will find in the long run only hatred, loneliness, despair, rage, ruin, and decay. But look for Christ and you will find Him, and with Him everything else thrown in.[3]

This is precisely what happens at Pentecost as it did in the desert at the end of the book of Exodus. Once sin-guilt is atoned for and God's people take on the heart posture of humility, servanthood, and obedience, he shares his presence, his very glory with his people. And when this happens, order is restored to the creation and the people of God become the window through which the world can witness YAHWEH who is holy, and whose glory fills the earth (Isa 6:3).

But how is Pentecost *different* from the exodus? It's different in that now the Temple has been relocated, or redefined. It was once a building, and now it is the living Temple of the corporate body of believers. This is what Jesus taught. This is what Jesus was saying in John 2. We dealt with this passage earlier when we mentioned the wedding at Cana. We said that Jesus turned water into wine using stone jars used for ceremonial purification. We said that this symbolized the fact that Jesus came to offer an *internal*

---

3. Lewis, *Mere Christianity*, 175.

cleansing. This concept, then, links up with the narrative of the cleansing of the Temple in the same chapter of John. It's not coincidence that these two stories are back-to-back in John's gospel.

Note the details of the text. The first thing John tells us is that this occurs during the time of Passover (John 2:13). This means that there is a parallel between what Christ is doing here and what happened in the exodus. Jesus drives out the moneychangers and then the Jews challenge him. They ask him:

> "What sign do you show us for doing these things?" Jesus answered them, "Destroy this temple, and in three days I will raise it up." The Jews then said, "It has taken forty-six years to build this temple, and will you raise it up in three days?" But he was speaking about the temple of his body (John 2:18–21).

Jesus is redefining the temple and teaching that he has come to cleanse the temple. This is further explained with the object lesson from the wedding at Cana. This means that he has come for an internal cleansing. What's the purpose of that cleansing? The same purpose as for cleansing the Tabernacle in the desert: to receive the *kābôḏ ʾĕlōhîm* so that order is restored to the creation through his chosen people.

This is the narrative, the deeply rich Old Testament theological heritage behind all of Paul's language about the corporate people of God being the Temple of God.[4] We see this especially at the end of Ephesians 2 where Paul says:

> For through him we both have access in one Spirit to the Father. So then you are no longer strangers and aliens, but you are fellow citizens with saints and members of the household of God, built on the foundation of the apostles and prophets, Christ Jesus himself being the cornerstone, in whom the whole structure, being joined together, grows into a holy temple in the Lord. In him you also are being built together into a dwelling place for God by the Spirit (Eph 2:18–22).

There are two things that are especially noteworthy about what Paul is saying here. The first is the importance of the Holy Spirit in the whole matter of making the corporate people of God his dwelling place. The image of tongues of fire over the heads of the apostles in Acts 2 shows us that God's special presence is made into the dwelling place of the Holy Spirit. At the

---

4. For an excellent treatment of issue see Beale, *The Temple and the Church's Mission.*

same time, it is the *collective people of God together who make up the Temple, not merely the individual.* The importance of this is tied directly to the second noteworthy item about what Paul's saying and that is the access to the promises of Abraham for Gentile believers in Jesus. This is the larger point that Paul is indeed making in this passage of Scripture. Paul is emphasizing, once again, that those "who were far off" were brought near through Jesus and that this is the great mystery of the Gospel.

What we have here is a perfect example of how Paul interweaves his ecclesiology, soteriology, eschatology, and Christology These things are inseparable for Paul. This is the point that we've been making since the very beginning. This is the point that the NP helps us grasp. And this is the point that holiness doctrine cannot fail to account for. The bottom line is that we cannot think about holiness without *Christ being in the center and not the individual believer* (Christology). And at the same time, we cannot think about holiness without consideration of the *collective and corporate nature of the body of Christ working together, by the power of the Holy Spirit, to complete the Great Commission in the image of Christ* (ecclesiology). And finally, we cannot think about holiness without taking into account that the kingdom that is being launched through the work of Christ and his Bride is both now and not yet (eschatology). At the center of all of this is the restoration of *both* the ontological and vocational dimension of the image of God being at the exact center of God's World Renewal Plan for the sake of *his presence, his glory being restored in the earth as was originally intended.* This is *salvation in fresh perspective.*

The Kingdom and the Resurrection

It is at the point where these dimensions converge that the concept of kingdom comes to the front of our thinking. Definitions and descriptions of the kingdom of God have been explored thoroughly in other places so there's no need to re-cover all of that ground here.[5] What I do wish to explore, however, is precisely how the biblical notion of the kingdom of God fits into the bigger picture of God's World Renewal Plan with a particular attention lent to holiness. With this, we will simply see a summary of what we have been talking about all along in resituating the biblical doctrine of salvation in its proper context.

5. For a solid engagement of the *biblical* notion of the kingdom of God in a contemporary context see McKnight, *Kingdom Conspiracy.*

The Lordship of Jesus, The Servant King

First off, inherent to the notion of the kingdom of God is the Lordship of Jesus Christ. Christ is king. Complementary to this idea is the concept of the servanthood of believers. One cannot be a part of the covenant people of God who have access to the promises of God made to Israel while being separated from the lordship of the Messiah. Believers are *submitted and conformed to his will.* Interestingly, conforming to a servant posture is not only conforming to the will of Jesus, but also to the very character of Jesus. This is why Paul begins his wonderful statement in Philippians 2:1–11 with the commend to "have this mind among yourselves, which is yours in Christ Jesus . . ." Being a servant is not only being obedient to Christ, but also being *like* Christ in his very servanthood. We dealt in detail with this issue in chapter 3.

Collective Kingdom Citizens and The Corporate Body

When people enter into a saving relationship with Jesus they do so *via* the covenant. They not only enter into a covenant with Jesus; they simultaneously enter into a covenant with God's people. When the individual believer conforms his or her life after the character of Christ in full obedience by means of the Holy Spirit, *the kingdom of God becomes a part of them.* The kingdom of God is manifest in their hearts because it is there that King Jesus reigns as is evidenced in the heart-posture and behavior of the believer.

While the kingdom of God certainly is manifest in individual believers, it finds its full expression in the corporate body of Christ. Paul is insistent that the work of Christ is a reconciling work. What Jesus did on the cross is eliminate the hostility between man and God as well as man and man. Jesus brings peace; this means that the convergence of sanctification and the coming kingdom is something collective, corporate, and reconciling. Our biblical doctrine of holiness must account for this feature of the kingdom and Christ's work. This means that the church as the body of Christ carries and continues the work of Christ *via* its obedience to the Great Commission. This is the holiness dimension of salvation in its vocational dimension.

The Kingdom is Now, but Not Yet

The third and final feature of kingdom that I want to bring to the front is that the kingdom is now but not yet (the eschatological dimension of the kingdom). Jesus' rule has been established through the cross and resurrection. Through faith in Jesus people are able to become citizens of the kingdom. At the same time, the kingdom is *not yet*. Jesus has yet to pronounce final judgment. Not only this, but Jesus has also yet to establish his *physical kingdom* on earth where his people no longer suffer the pains of sin and death and the ongoing, earthly rule of evil. Yes, Jesus has overthrown the powers of this world and he has overcome the principalities and authorities of the old evil age. And yet, kingdom citizens get cancer. Kingdom citizens suffer, just as he did. The messianic people are persecuted just as he was. All of this evidences that while Christ has gained victory through the cross, the Evil One still reigns on earth. The final and complete destruction of the Evil One is yet to come.

Two camps have emerged in attempts to reconcile the paradox of the kingdom now, but not yet. The first camp is *triumphalism* and the second *defeatism*. Triumphalism has made the mistake of neglecting, and sometimes altogether ignoring, the *not yet* dimension of the kingdom. Triumphalism teaches that because of Christ's victory, God's people are never to suffer. They teach that the *fullness* of the kingdom is *now*. Not only that, if God's people do suffer it is because of sin, or a lack of faith. This goes hand-in-handwith economic status as well. God, according to triumphalism, wills his people to not only have health, but also wealth and prosperity. Kingdom citizens aren't poor because God reigns through Jesus, and God certainly doesn't wish his people to be poor. Poverty, then, must be the consequence of sin. This position, once again, altogether dismisses that New Testament writers taught that while the kingdom is now, *it is also not yet*. The fullness of the kingdom of God has yet to arrive.

On the other side of the same coin we have defeatism. Defeatism over-emphasizes the *not yet* dimension of the kingdom and neglects the *now*. Defeatism has a tendency to take a posture that says something like, "Well, until Christ's return, I will live the best I can, as a sinner enslaved to sin in this body of sin until I die or until Christ's return, whichever comes first." Defeatism, like Luther, takes Romans 7 to be a description of the average Christian life by which we should set our expectations. On this matter E. P. Sanders writes,

Luther saw the Christian life as summed up in Romans 7:21, "I find it to be a law that when I want to do right, evil lies close at hand," whereas Paul thought that this was the plight from which people were freed through Christ (Rom. 7:24; 8:1–8). "You," he wrote, "are note in the Flesh, you are in the Spirit"; and those in the Spirit, he fought, did not do the sinful deeds "of the Flesh" (Rom. 8:9–17; Gal. 5:16–24).[6]

Defeatism, like Luther, forgets to read Romans 8. This is a mistake. Yes, we are to suffer now because the fullness of the kingdom has yet to arrive; however, the kingdom *has, in fact, been launched and deliverance begins today.* Something else that defeatism tragically misses is that Christ has commissioned his church to be the agent by which the kingdom is established on earth. Defeatism has the tendency to neglect the mission, the vocational dynamic of salvation.

Both defeatism and triumphalism have their problems. At the same time, they share one problem and that is that both focus on *me.* What do I mean by this? I mean that the starting point for salvation is what *Christ has done* and will do for the believer as opposed to the focus being on what Christ does *through* the believer for *himself.* There is a tragic neglect of the critically important dimension of Christ *through me.* In terms of prepositions, we can talk about what Christ does *for* the church, what Christ does *to* the church, what Christ does *in* the church, and what Christ does *through the church for himself.* This is a theme that we see in the book of Jeremiah where God promises through the prophet Jeremiah that he will redeem rebellious Israel, not for their sake but for his own. The shared error of defeatism and triumphalism is that salvation is *understood with the believer as the primary point of reference rather than with Jesus and the Holy Trinity as the primary point of referencefor God's great salvation..* We will also see that this can stand as a valid critique of the more traditional ways of talking about holiness. We have a habit of talking about holiness with ourselves being the primary point of reference. This, once again, isn't all bad, but it is out of balance and needs correction. We will flesh this out a bit more below.

So how can we properly, from within a strong biblical framework, bring these two realities of now but not yet together? Jesus reigns, yet evil still seems to greatly prevail. How is it that the triumph is now, but not yet? Can it be truly considered "triumph" while the war still seems to be

6. Sanders, *Paul*, 58.

raging on? "Victory?" you may ask. When Christians are persecuted and the world's conscience seems to be deteriorating? How can this be?

These questions are essentially trying to get at a biblical eschatology in which Paul's understanding of holiness is properly placed. In other words, all of this sets the framework for correctly placing Paul's understanding of holiness and salvation. It is in this eschatological context that we are able to explore how Paul thought about things like sin in believers, the transformation of the heart, and the gradual manifestation of the kingdom of God through the church by means of the Holy Spirit.

The fact that the kingdom is now and not yet means that salvation is dynamic. Salvation, like the kingdom, is for a people and through a people all at once. The resurrection of Jesus is the launching of the new creation right in the middle of history and those who are in Christ are both working towards the expansion of Christ's reign in the creation while simultaneously waiting his return.

Each of these features of the kingdom that we have briefly touched upon here flows from the work of the cross. The cross is central. The cross is the means through which all of this is possible precisely because the cross deals with the sin-guilt problem tied to the moral autonomy of humanity that results in death. The servanthood of Jesus functions, then, not only as an example of the vocational dimension of holiness but also the very atoning work that reconciles the Creator to the creation and vice versa.

The Resurrection Is Not About Dying and Going to Heaven

With the World Renewal Plan properly in perspective, we are able to see that the bodily resurrection of Jesus is not about the Christian notion of dying and going to heaven. Unfortunately there is a gross misunderstanding about the notion of dying and going to heaven being central to salvation. The first thing that our minds go to about the resurrection is that it's somehow illustrative of dying and going to heaven, because, after all, Jesus did eventually go to heaven after his resurrection (the Ascension). This is not what it's about.[7]

The resurrection is ultimately all about the renewal of creation. It is about the launching of the New Creation as the ultimate fulfillment of God's World Renewal Plan. What does that mean? Well, it all comes down

---

7. See Witherington, *Revelation* and Wright, *Surprised by Hope.*

to God's faithfulness, God's faithfulness to Israel as their Patron Deity, and God's faithfulness to the creation as its Creator.

We all know that there is a problem with the creation. This is one of the easiest points of Christian theology to argue with non-believers. Just consider for a moment the state of affairs on earth and it becomes apparent that something is wrong. Injustice in the world, greed, poverty, dishonesty, cheating, adultery, along with hurricanes, tornadoes, earthquakes, sickness, disease, death; they are all signs of the problem.

As the Creator, God has committed to be faithful to solve these problems (even though the problems are the result of humanity's infidelity). His strategy is to create all over again. God's World Renewal Plan centers on reconciliation *and* rebirth. God, through the resurrection of Jesus, demonstrates to the world that he is launching a New Creation. This old creation of sin, decay, corruption, and death is slowly passing away and there is a new age to come, a new age of liberation and complete wholeness. The resurrection is all about the new creation as the finishing touch of God's World Renewal Plan.

Conclusion: The Faithfulness of God: Holiness

All along the way we have been reorienting the notion of salvation around the faithfulness of God to Israel and the creation. I've done this because this is what the New Testament (and the NP) does. The NP talks about Christ's work on the cross, Jesus as the Messiah, as beginning the atoning work of God that redeems believers from sin-guilt (justification). This work is the ultimate act of God's faithfulness to both Israel as well as to the rest of the *cosmos*. I, however, wish to take this one step further and say that the faithfulness of God is *holiness*.

This isn't to deny or discount justification as a part of the greater picture of God's World Renewal Plan being the expression of his faithfulness; however, it is to suggest that focusing on justification alone is incomplete. The NP has reoriented readers of the New Testament to the fact that the New Testament grows out the theological heritage of the Old Testament; we cannot read the New Testament severed from its Old Testament roots. I have been making this case all along, but with special emphasis on the work of atonement being preparatory for the *return of the glory/presence of God in the midst of his people*. The blood of the covenant, the atoning work of Christ, and justification, is the *means* for a greater goal, and that is the reestablishment of God's righteous reign on earth as it was originally intended. This is the kingdom of God. In the kingdom, believers in Jesus conform to his very image (sanctification) by taking the form of a servant (Phil 2 and Isa 52:13—53:12) and obeying his every command. This is *holiness* in fresh perspective.

God was faithful to his promises to Israel. The greatest promise was that they would be his people and he would be their God. This promise encapsulates all other promises; the promise to be the people of God is to share his image, to partake in his very character. Israel received the promise that they would be "a chosen race, a royal priesthood, a holy nation, a people for his own possession" (1 Pet 2:9). They were called to be the true Israel by sharing God's nature and reflecting his glory into the creation. The great promise was to be in communion with God in *holiness*. Through Jesus, this promise is answered. The manifestation of the holiness of the people of God is the ultimate expression of the faithfulness of God to Israel and to the *cosmos*.

Conclusion

Salvation in Its Proper Eschatological Framework

THE LORD OF THE Rings trilogy is one of my favorite film series. I do have to admit, however, that it took me quite a while to gain an appreciation for the films. In looking back on the films I've been troubled by one of the episodes at the very end of the movie. Frodo and Sam have finally accomplished their mission by taking the ring to Mordor after a long, hard journey. The pain, frustration, challenge and difficulty they had to face to take the ring to Mordor across hundreds if not thousands of miles of the frightening land of Middle Earth is immeasurable. Middle Earth is a land of all sorts of creatures, both benevolent and evil. It is a land of both harsh and welcoming landscapes. There are meadows and plowed field as well as jagged rocks, cliffs, and marshes. In the midst of all of this, Middle Earth is war-struck. There are forces of evil mobilizing to take over Middle Earth while the forces of good fight to defend what is theirs. Frodo and Sam not only face harsh landscapes and various creatures, but battlelands.

At the end of the third and last installment of the trilogy (*The Return of the King*), Frodo and Sam lay exhausted and relieved from their journey on a molten rock on the side of an erupting volcano so as to escape being destroyed by the lava that is pouring out of the top of the volcano. As they lie there, they drift into a dreamlike state out of both exhaustion and relief that their journey has finally come to a close. Just then, two giant eagles swoop down and gently grip Frodo and Sam in their talons and lift them off the rock to take them home and to escape the threat of the lava. I thought, "Now wait a minute, why didn't they just hitch a ride from these birds to Mordor to begin with? That would have enabled them to destroy the ring in one fell swoop and they wouldn't have had to suffer through the agonizing journey to Mordor! No Gollum, no orcs, no bogs or marshes, no cliff climbing, no massive spiders, no battles, no rivers, it could have been done just like that!"

Tolkien has no clever answer for us to this question. I suppose it could have happened that way; however, if it did, *then there would be no story*, and if we have no story, then we have nothing. I came to realize that the point of the story is not just destroying the ring, the point of the story is transformation. Along with this, we find a beautiful allegory of how evil is overcome in the world by ordinary people (like Hobbits) and how ordinary people become extraordinary people by taking on the cause of the *other* when they would really rather remain comfortably in their armchairs and gardens at home drinking tea and ale. This adventure, which illustrates sacrifice for a greater cause, demonstrates how people change; people change through trial.

We can turn around and ask a similar question at this point: why didn't Jesus simply come and do it all at once? Why didn't he die on the cross, resurrect, then pronounce final judgment and thereby put an end, once and for all, to the old evil age? Why wait? How can we make sense of this? Why allow persecution? Why allow evil to persist for another (at least) two thousand years? We are not alone in trying to deal with this dilemma. These were dimensions of Paul's thought as well, and herein lay the key to understanding salvation and the kingdom according to Paul. So much of what Paul and other NT writers wrote was dealing with the problem of persecution. What a dilemma indeed! If Jesus ruled over the universe as the true Son of God, why did Caesar's rule not come to an end? Why was the church rejected by the culture? As Paul responds to these issues in the church, his doctrine of salvation is revealed. It is evident, then that for Paul, salvation, holiness, and eschatology go hand in hand.

To get a firmer grasp on this, I find it helpful to consider the teachings of Jesus about the kingdom. Jesus, over and over again, emphasized one particular dynamic about the kingdom and that is that it would develop and grow *over time and through trials and difficulty.* The kingdom, contrary to belief among Jesus' contemporaries, would not be established overnight. The kingdom is like a tree; it grows so slow that its growth, at times, can hardly be perceived. It is gradual and organic. When we take this agricultural metaphor a bit further, we're able to get a better idea of what was happening through Jesus' earthly ministry. It is almost as if Jesus' earthly ministry was to, like the farmer, carryout the crucial preparations to create the right conditions for growth. Jesus came to cut down old trees and remove the old, rotten and corrupted root system in order to plant a new one. He came to prepare the soil, level the ground and remove the weeds and stones. Jesus came to plant the perfect seed in the perfect context so that it could grow into something entirely new, stable, and strong even in the midst of the harsh forces of nature.

This metaphor is not original. We read about a similar parable in Isaiah 5. There is a different slant, however, in Isaiah's parable. Isaiah compares Israel and her relationship to YAHWEH with a vineyard and its owner. God is the owner and Israel is the vineyard. The owner went through all the pains of doing it right. He removed the rocks from the field, and he built a wall and a watchtower. He chose the finest seeds for planting. After all the long and painstaking preparations, he planted his vineyard. Much to his disappointment, the vineyard produced sour grapes. The vineyard was corrupt. As a result the owner decides to let the forces of nature take over the vineyard. He lets it go. Thus it was with Israel. God was faithful and Israel was not.

Now, in Jesus, regardless of Israel's faithfulness, God remains faithful to his promise to Israel. He starts yet another garden project. He uproots the old and plants a new kingdom. This is the idea tied up in the image of Jesus cleansing the temple and cursing the fig tree (Matt 21:12–22). This is also the nature of Jesus' language in describing the messianic kingdom (Matt 13). Jesus says the kingdom is like a sower of seed, like a field that is threatened by thorns, like a mustard seed that grows *slowly* into a tree. He also says that it is like leaven that makes the entire lump expand *over time*. Jesus makes it clear that the kingdom is something that takes time and process.

We see this in the Old Testament as well, specifically in the exodus and wilderness wanderings. Israel does not go right from redemption from Egypt to the Promised Land. They are slaves who must learn to be a true *nation*. They need the law of God to guide and direct them in what it is to be God's people. They must learn and in order to learn they must trust.

Not only that, but why didn't God, by his miraculous power, just walk Israel right out of Egypt, through the desert, and into Canaan? Why the plagues? Why the trials of the desert? Why the grumblings? Why the manna and the water from the rock? *You see, God orchestrates the coming of his kingdom with human participation. God chooses to do his work through human agents. He allows these things because this is the stuff of human transformation and growth.* God waited for Moses to cry out for help before dividing the Red Sea. Why not simply tell Moses in advance, "Now, Moses, when you arrive at the Red Sea, don't worry, I'll divide it for you." No! God waits for Moses to turn to God and say, "What do I do now?!" God waits for Moses because he invites human participation. Everything must happen within the framework of human–divine fellowship, even if that fellowship takes the form of argument.

We could identify further examples, but this is adequate to make a most important point about salvation, the kingdom, and holiness. The point is this: if Jesus constantly emphasized that the kingdom grows over time, then why has the Western church's emphasis on salvation been the importance of the punctiliar event of justification? This event is undoubtedly important. However, we are in great danger when we forget that the thrust of Jesus' teaching about the kingdom is its *progressive.*

This reality resonates with other stories in Scripture. Take Abraham, for example. Did the story of Abraham end after he believed God and was reckoned as righteous because of it? No! That is the beauty of the story of Abraham. The beauty of it is that Abraham and God grow in relationship together over time. Abraham's faith, over time, grows deeper and deeper to the point where he is ready to sacrifice that which is most valuable to him, a gift from God, in fact, for the sake of his relationship with YAHWEH. For Abraham, God's presence is more important than God's presents. At first, it is likely that Abraham obeys God for what he believes God is able to do for him. By the end of the Abraham narrative, however, Abraham obeys God because he loves and fears God for who he is.

Peter is another example. Peter and Jesus had ups and downs. In one moment Peter makes his famous confession, and in the very next Jesus calls him Satan. In a similar fashion, in one moment Peter draws his sword and slices off Malchus' servant's ear (Matt 26:51) in defense of Jesus and in the very next he is denying him (Matt 26:70). Granted, these failures take place prior to Pentecost; however, the New Testament makes clear that Peter was by no means faultless after Pentecost either (see the story of Cornelius in Acts 10 as well as Paul's exhortation of Peter (Gal 2:11)). The point here is not that we will always have faults, although I do believe this is the case. The point is, however, that *salvation is a relationship, and justification is the initial basis of that relationship and sanctification is the lengthy, progressive playing out of that relationship.* I can't emphasize this enough. This relationship is the kingdom, as it exists in the hearts of the church. The kingdom is launched through the cross (justification) and grows and develops over time, in the church through the work of the Spirit of Christ.

Consider John the Baptist. At the beginning part of John's ministry, he was Jesus' number one advocate. "He preached saying, 'After me comes he who is mightier than I, the strap of whose sandals I am not worth to stoop down and untie. I have baptized you with water, but he will baptize you with the Holy Spirit'" (Mark 1:7–8). Then, a short time later, when John sits in prison with a death sentence (what hardly seems to be a proper reward for faithfulness to Jesus), he sends messengers to Jesus to ask a simple question: "Are you the one who is to come, or shall we look for another?" (Matt 11:3). What a change! What has happened to John's faith? Hardship and trial is the context in which John is able to see with great clarity the limits of his faith in Jesus for the sake of further growth. God is showing him his weakness. But why? He shows him his weakness to make him stronger—to sanctify him. This is salvation in fresh perspective.

We see with this that salvation, while being punctiliar, is also a process. *Salvation is the process of God's kingdom come on earth* (Matt 6:10). Salvation is how, through our faith in Jesus, the Holy Spirit probes the inner depths of our hearts to reveal to us where we are weak and where we need further growth. The Holy Spirit makes us the fully human people we are created to be. What is crucial in all of this is that it all happens within the context of *intimate personal relationship*.

I recently heard an interesting interpretation of the closing of the book of Job. Many interpreters have suggested that Job's friends got it all wrong. That may be and I'm still very sympathetic to this interpretation. At the same time, this new interpretation suggested that yes, they did get it wrong in suggesting that Job's suffering was the consequence of sin; however, the rest of what they had to say wasn't all that bad. What set Job apart from them, however, is that Job spoke *to God about it while his friends simply spoke to each other*. What I love about this interpretation is that it suggests that what's most important is that we are in real, sincere, and authentic dialogue with the Father. Whether or not we get all our Ts crossed right or not is, certainly, important; however, what is most important is a heart that is diligently, and with sincerity, seeking after God through Jesus.

What is the significance of this? This highlights the fact that this builds relationship and it is in the context of relationship that salvation occurs. Not only that, but salvation also occurs in relationship *for relationship*. This all reflects the triune nature of God. We are in error if we think that the goal of salvation is sanctification. We are correct, however, to think that the goal of salvation is sanctification when sanctification is defined as *thy kingdom come* via *personal relationship*.

This, I believe, is why the kingdom is like a tree that grows slowly over time. Relationships take time. As humans, we *know* the time it takes to build trust. I like to compare this dynamic to a parent, who with great patience, teaches his/her child to do something new, like reading, or riding a bike. The first thing we note is that it is not the task that is most important, but the relationship. Second, because of the relationship, the parent patiently pushes, challenges, and grows the child in his/her understanding *so that the child can develop into all that he or she is capable of being*. This is the kingdom. Certainly, the parent can do all the homework for the child, but what a great disservice! In much the same way, God created humanity with great potential. Sin destroys this feature of humanness. God's will is to restore our humanness. God teaches, guides, and directs us into all that he has created us to be as humans. This is his ministry to humanity. This takes time and requires a relationship. God, like a parent, finds great joy in watching us grow, even if it requires great pain. This is why Israel needed the desert, John needed prison, and we need difficulty and challenge in order to grow.

Too often we sadly exchange this rich, biblical understanding of the kingdom of God and holiness for something cheap that is expressed in questions like, "have you sinned today?" This isn't a bad question, per se, but it does tend to *depersonalize* the nature of sanctification and kingdom. God is not an accountant, but a Father. Sin is something deeply personal, not *merely* the violation of a rule.

I wish to close with this from Oswald Chambers:

> Christian perfection is not, and never can be, human perfection. Christian perfection is the perfection of a relationship to God which shows itself amid the irrelevancies of human life. When you obey the call of Jesus Christ, the first thing that strikes you is the irrelevancy of the things you have to do, and the next thing that strikes you is the fact that other people seem to be living perfectly consistent lives. Such lives are apt to leave you with the idea that God is unnecessary, by human effort and devotion we can reach the standard God wants. In a fallen world this can never be done. I am called to live in perfect relation to God so that my life produces a longing after God in other lives, not admiration for myself. Thoughts about myself hinder my usefulness to God. God is not

after perfecting me to be a specimen in His show-room; He is getting me to the place where He can use me. Let Him do what He
likes.[1]

1. Chambers, *My Utmost for His Highest*, Dec. 2.

Suggested Reading

Allison, Dale. *The New Moses: A Matthean Typology*. Eugene: Wipf & Stock, 2013.

Bateman, Herbert W., IV, Darrell L. Bock, and Gordon H. Johnston. *Jesus the Messiah: Tracing the Promises, Expectations, and Coming of Israel's King*. Grand Rapids: Kregel Academic, 2012.

Beker, J. C. *Paul the Apostle: The Triumph of God in Life and Thought*. Philadelphia: Fortress, 1980.

Bird, Michael F. *Are you the One Who Is to Come? The Historical Jesus and the Messianic Question*. Grand Rapids: Baker Academic, 2009.

———. *Introducing Paul: The Man, His Mission, and His Message*. Downers Grove, IL: InterVarsity, 2008.

———. *The Saving Righteousness of God: Studies in Paul, Justification, and the New Perspective*. Milton Keynes, UK: Paternoster, 2007.

Bird, Michael F., and Preston M. Sprinkle, eds. *The Faith of Jesus Christ: Exegetical, Biblical, and Theological Studies*. Milton Keynes, UK: Paternoster, 2010.

Cambell, Douglas A. *The Quest for Paul's Gospel: A Suggested Strategy*. London: T. & T. Clark, 2005.

Chilton, Bruce, and Jacob Neusner. *Judaism in the New Testament: Practices and Beliefs*. London: Routlege, 1995.

Collins, John J. *The Scepter and the Star: The Messiahs of the Dead Sea Scrolls and Other Ancient Literature*. New York: Doubleday, 1995.

Dunn, James D. G. *Beginning from Jerusalem*. Grand Rapids: Eerdmans, 2008.

———. *The Cambridge Companion to St. Paul*. Cambridge: Cambridge University Press, 2003.

———. *The Historical Jesus in Recent Research*. Warsaw: Eisenbrauns, 2006.

———. *Jesus, Paul and the Gospels*. Grand Rapids: Eerdmans, 2001.

———. *Jesus Remembered: Christianity in the Making*. Vol. 1. Grand Rapids: Eerdmans, 2003.

———. *A New Perspective on Jesus: What the Quest for the Historical Jesus Missed*. Grand Rapids: Baker Academic, 2005.

———. *The New Perspective on Paul: Collected Essays*. Grand Rapids: Eerdmans, 2007.

———. *The Theology of Paul the Apostle*. Grand Rapids: Eerdmans, 2006.

Hays, Richard B. *Echoes of Scripture in the Letters of Paul*. New Haven, CT: Yale University Press, 1993.

Horsley, Richard. *The Prophet Jesus and the Renewal of Israel: Moving Beyond A Diversionary Debate*. Grand Rapids: Eerdmans, 2012.

McKnight, Scot. *The King Jesus Gospel: The Original Good News Revisited*. Grand Rapids: Zondervan, 2011.

———. *Kingdom Conspiracy: Returning to the Radical Mission of the Local Church*. Grand Rapids: Brazos, 2014.

Oswalt, John. *Exodus: The Way Out*. Anderson, IN: Warner, 2013.

Perrin, Nicholas, and Richard B. Hays, eds. *Jesus, Paul and the People of God: A Theological Dialogue with N. T. Wright*. London: SPCK, 2011.

Porter, Stanley E. *The Messiah in the Old and New Testaments*. Grand Rapids: Eerdmans, 2007.

Porter, Stanley E., and Cynthia Long Westfall. *Empire in the New Testament*. Eugene, OR: Wipf & Stock, 2011.

Sanders, E. P. *The Historical Figure of Jesus*. London: Penguin, 1993.

———. *Jesus and Judaism*. London: SCM, 1985.

———. *Paul, the Law, and the Jewish People*. Minneapolis: Fortress, 1983.

Thiselton, Anthony C. *The Living Paul: Introduction to the Apostle and His Thought*. London: SPCK, 2009.

Witherington, Ben, III. *Invitation to the New Testament: First Things*. Oxford: Oxford University Press, 2012.

———. *The Many Faces of the Christ: The Christologies of the New Testament and Beyond*. New York: Crossroad, 1998.

———. *Revelation and the End Times Participant's Guide: Unraveling God's Message of Hope*. Nashville: Abingdon, 2010.

Wright, Christopher J. H. *Knowing Jesus Through the Old Testament*. Downers Grove, IL: InterVarsity, 1992.

Wright, N. T. *How God Became King*. New York: HarperOne, 2012.

———. *Jesus and the Victory of God*. London: SPCK, 1996.

———. *Justification: God's Plan, Paul's Vision*. Downers Grove, IL: InterVarsity, 2009.

———. *The New Testament and the People of God*. Minneapolis: Fortress, 1992.

———. *Paul and His Recent Interpreters*. Minneapolis: Fortress, 2014.

———. *Paul and the Faithfulness of God*. Minneapolis: Fortress, 2013.

———. *Paul In Fresh Perspective*. Minneapolis: Fortress, 2009.

———, ed. *Pauline Perspectives: Essays on Paul, 1978–2013*. Minneapolis: Fortress, 2013.

Bibliography

Adams, Edward. *Parallel Lives of Jesus: Four Gospels, One Story*. London: SPCK, 2011.

Alexander, T. Desmond, and Brian Rosner, eds. *New Dictionary of Biblical Theology*. Downers Grove, IL: InterVarsity, 2000.

Allison, Dale C., Jr. *The New Moses: A Matthean Typology*. Edinburgh: T. & T. Clark, 1993.

Balla, P. "Challenges to Biblical Theology." In *New Dictionary of Biblical Theology*, edited by T. Desmond Alexander and Brian S. Rosner, 20–27. Downers Grove, IL: InterVarsity, 2000.

Beale, G. K. *The Temple and the Church's Mission: A Biblical Theology of the Dwelling Place of God*. Edited by D. A. Carson. New Studies in Biblical Theology. Downers Grove, IL: InterVarsity, 2004.

Berlin, Adele. "Reading Biblical Poetry." In *The Jewish Study Bible*, edited by Adele Berlin and Marc Z. Brettler, 2184–91. Oxford: Oxford University Press, 2004.

Berlin, Adele, and Marc Z. Brettler, eds. *The Jewish Study Bible*. Oxford: Oxford University Press, 2004.

Bird, Michael. *The Gospel of the Lord: How the Early Church Wrote the Story of Jesus*. Grand Rapids: Eerdmans, 2014.

———. *Introducing Paul: The Man, His Mission, and His Message*. Downers Grove, IL: InterVarsity, 2008.

Block, Daniel I. "My Servant David: Ancient Israel's Vision of the Messiah." In *Israel's Messiah in the Bible and the Dead Sea Scrolls*, edited by Richard S. Hess and M. Daniel Carroll R., 17–56. Grand Rapids: Baker Academic, 2003.

Blomberg, Craig L. *Contagious Holiness: Jesus' Meals with Sinners*. Edited by D. A. Carson. New Studies in Biblical Theology. Downers Grove, IL: InterVarsity, 2005.

Brunson, Andrew C. *Psalm 118 in the Gospel of John: An Intertextual Study on the New Exodus Pattern in the Theology of John*. Tübingen: Mohr, 2003.

Bock, Darrell L. *The Mission Gospels: Unearthing the Truth Behind Alternative Christianities*. Nashville: Nelson, 2006.

Chambers, Oswald. *My Utmost for His Highest: Selections for the Year*. Grand Rapids: Marshall Pickering, 1986.

Charlesworth, James, ed. *Qumran-Messianism: Studies on the Messianic Expectations in the Dead Sea Scrolls*. Tübingen: Mohr, 1998.

Chilton, Bruce, and Jacob Neusner. *Judaism in the New Testament: Practices and Beliefs*. London: Routlege, 1995.

Collins, John J. *The Scepter and the Star: The Messiahs of the Dead Sea Scrolls and Other Ancient Literature*. New York: Doubleday, 1995.

De Claissé-Walford, Nancy, Rolf A. Jacobson, and Beth LaNeel Tanner. *The Book of Psalms*. New International Commentary on the Old Testament. Grand Rapids: Eerdmans, 2014.

Dunn, James D. G. *Jesus Rememberd*. Vol. 1, *Christianity in the Making*. Grand Rapids, Eerdmans, 2003.

Elliot, Mark Adam. *The Survivors of Israel: A Reconsideration of the Theology of Pre-Christian Judaism*. Grand Rapids: Eerdmans, 2000.

Evans, Craig A. "King Jesus and His Ambassadors." In *Empire in the New Testament*, edited by Stanley E. Porter and Cynthia Long Westfall, 120–39. Eugene, OR: Wipf & Sock, 2011.

———. "The Messiah in the Dead Sea Scrolls." In *Israel's Messiah in the Bible and the Dead Sea Scrolls*, edited by Richard S. Hess and M. Daniel Carroll R., 85–102. Grand Rapids: Baker Academic, 2003.

Ferguson, Everett. *The Church of Christ: A Biblical Ecclesiology for Today*. Grand Rapids: Eerdmans, 1996.

Hamilton, Victor. *Exodus: An Exegetical Commentary*. Grand Rapids: Baker Academic, 2011.

Harris, R. Laird, ed. *Theological Wordbook of the Old Testament*. Chicago: Moody Bible Institute, 1980.

Hess, Richard S., and M. Daniel Carroll R. *Israel's Messiah in the Bible and the Dead Sea Scrolls*. Grand Rapids: Baker Academic, 2003.

Käsemann, Ernst. *Commentary on Romans*. Translated by Geoffrey W. Bromiley. Grand Rapids: Eerdmans, 1980.

Keener, Craig S. *The Gospel of Matthew: A Socio-Rhetorical Commentary*. Grand Rapids: Eerdmans, 2009.

Keesmaat, Sylvia C. *Paul and His Story: (Re)Interpreting the Exodus Tradition*. Journal for the Study of the New Testament Supplement Series 181. Sheffield: Sheffield Academic Press, 1999.

Keller, Timothy. *Jesus the King: Understanding the Life and Death of the Son of God*. New York: Riverhead, 2013.

Koehler, Ludwig, Walter Baumgartner, M. E. J Richardson, and Johann Jakob Stamm. *The Hebrew and Aramaic Lexicon of the Old Testament*. Electronic ed. Leiden: Brill, 1999.

Koester, Helmut. *From Jesus to the Gospels: Interpreting the New Testament in Its Context*. Minneapolis: Fortress, 2007.

Levenson, Jon D. *Sinai and Zion: An Entry into the Jewish Bible*. New York: HarperOne, 1987.

Lewis, C. S. *Mere Christianity*. New York: Macmillan, 1958.

———. *The Problem of Pain*. San Francisco: HarperCollins, 2001.

McKnight, Scot. *The King Jesus Gospel: The Original Good News Revisited*. Grand Rapids: Zondervan, 2011.

McMaan, C. T. "Meals as Type-Scences in the Gospel of Luke." PhD diss., Southern Baptist Theological Seminary, 1987.

Milkowski, Bill. *Jaco: The Extraordinary and Tragic Life of Jaco Pastorius*. Milwaukee: Hal Leonard, 2005.

Moo, Douglas J. *The Epistle to the Romans*. New International Commentary on the New Testament. Grand Rapids: Eerdmans, 1996.

Oswalt, John. *Called to the Holy: A Biblical Perspective*. Nappanee, IN: Evangel, 1999.

———. *Exodus: The Way Out*. Anderson, IN: Warner, 2013.

———. *Isaiah: The NIV Application Commentary*. Grand Rapids: Zondervan, 2003.

Perrin, Nicholas. "Jesus' Eschatology and Kingdom Ethics: Ever the Twain Shall Meet." In *Jesus, Paul, and the People of God: A Theological Dialogue with N. T. Wright*, edited by Nicholas Perrin and Richard B. Hays, 92–114. London: SPCK, 2011.

Peterson, David. *Possessed by God: A New Testament Theology of Sanctification and Holiness*. Edited by D. A. Carson. New Studies in Biblical Theology. Downers Grove, IL: InterVarsity, 1995.

Porter, Stanley E. *The Messiah in the Old and New Testaments*. Grand Rapids: Eerdmans, 2007.

Porter, Stanley E., and Cynthia L Westfall. *Empire in the New Testament*. Eugene: Wipf & Stock, 2011.

Richter, Sandra. *Epic of Eden: A Christian Entry into the World of the Old Testament*. Downers Grove, IL: InterVarsity, 2008.

Sanders, E. P. *The Historical Figure of Jesus*. London: Penguin, 1993.

———. *Jesus and Judaism*. London: SCM, 1985.

———. *Paul: A Very Short Introduction*. Oxford: Oxford University: 2001.

———. *Paul, the Law, and the Jewish People*. Minneapolis: Fortress, 1983.

Schreiner, Thomas R. *Romans*. Baker Exegetical Commentary on the New Testament. Grand Rapids: Baker, 1998.

Scott, James M. *Adoption as Sons of God*. Tübingen: Mohr, 1992.

Stuhlmacher, Peter, ed. *The Gospel and the Gospels*. Grand Rapids: Eerdmans, 1991.

———. *Paul's Letter to the Romans: A Commentary*. Translated by Scott J. Hafemann. Edinburgh: T. & T. Clark, 1994.

Thatcher, Tom. "'I have conquered the world': The Death of Jesus and the End of Empire in the Gospel of John." In *Empire in the New Testament*, edited by Stanley E. Porter and Cynthia Long Westfall, 140–63. Eugene, OR: Wipf & Stock, 2011.

Walton, John H. *The Lost World of Genesis One: Ancient Cosmology and Origins Debate*. Downers Grove, IL: InterVarsity, 2009.

Witherington, Ben, III. *Revelation and the End Times: Unraveling God's Message of Hope*. Nashville: Abingdon, 2010.

Witherington, Ben, III, and Darlene Hyatt. *Paul's Letter to the Romans: A Socio-Rhetorical Commentary*. Grand Rapids: Eerdmans, 2004.

Wright, N. T. *For All the Saints? Remembering the Christian Departed*. London: SPCK, 2003.

———. *How God Became King*. New York: HarperOne, 2012.

———. *Jesus and the Victory of God*. London: SPCK, 1996.

———. *Justification: God's Plan, Paul's Vision*. Downers Grove, IL: InterVarsity, 2009.

———. "The Letter to the Romans: Introduction, Commentary, and Reflections." In *The New Interpreter's Bible: A Commentary in Twelve Volumes*, edited by Leander E. Keck, 10:393–770. Nashville: Abingdon, 2002.

———. *The New Testament and the People of God*. Minneapolis: Fortress, 1992.

———. *Paul and His Recent Interpreters*. Minneapolis: Fortress, 2014.

———. *Paul and the Faithfulness of God*. Minneapolis: Fortress, 2013.

———. *Paul For Everyone: Romans Part 1, Chapters 1–8*. London: SPCK, 2004.

———. *Paul In Fresh Perspective*. Minneapolis: Fortress, 2009.

———, ed. *Pauline Perspectives: Essays on Paul, 1978–2013*. Minneapolis: Fortress, 2013.

————. "Poetry and Theology in Colossians 1.15–20." *New Testament Studies* 36 (1990) 444–68.

————. *Surprised by Hope.* New York: HarperCollins, 2008.

————. *Surprised by Scripture.* New York: HarperOne, 2014.

Ziesler, J. A. *Pauline Christianity.* Oxford: Oxford University Press, 1991.

Scripture Reference Index